HELLENIC STUDIES 33

GENOS DIKANIKON
Amateur and Professional Speech
in the Courtrooms of Classical Athens

D0873340

Other Titles in the Hellenic Studies Series

Plato's Rhapsody and Homer's Music
The Poetics of the Panathenaic Festival in Classical Athens

Labored in Papyrus Leaves
Perspectives on an Epigram Collection Attributed to Posidippus
(P.Mil.Vogl. VIII 309)

Helots and Their Masters in Laconia and Messenia
Histories, Ideologies, Structures

Archilochos Heros
The Cult of Poets in the Greek Polis

Master of the Game
Competition and Performance in Greek Poetry

Greek Ritual Poetics

Black Doves Speak
Herodotus and the Languages of Barbarians

Pointing at the Past
From Formula to Performance in Homeric Poetics

Homeric Conversation

The Life and Miracles of Thekla

Victim of the Muses
Poet as Scapegoat, Warrior and Hero
in Greco-Roman and Indo-European Myth and History

Amphoterōglossia
A Poetics of the Twelfth-Century Medieval Greek Novel

Priene (second edition)

Plato's Symposium
Issues in Interpretation and Reception

http://chs.harvard.edu

GENOS DIKANIKON
Amateur and Professional Speech in the Courtrooms of Classical Athens

Victor Bers

CENTER FOR HELLENIC STUDIES
Trustees for Harvard University
Washington, D.C.
Distributed by Harvard University Press
Cambridge, Massachusetts, and London, England
2009

Genos Dikanikon: Amateur and Professional Speech in the Courtrooms of Classical Athens
    by Victor Bers
Copyright © 2009 Center for Hellenic Studies, Trustees for Harvard University
All Rights Reserved.
Published by Center for Hellenic Studies, Trustees for Harvard University, Washington, DC.
Distributed by Harvard University Press, Cambridge, Massachusetts, and London, England
Printed in Ann Arbor, MI by Edwards Brothers, Inc.
Translations from George A. Kennedy, *Aristotle, On Rhetoric: A Theory of Civic Discourse*
    copyright © 1991 by Oxford University Press. Quoted by permission of Oxford University
    Press, Inc.
Translations from the Orators of Classical Greece series copyright © 1998–2007
    by University of Texas Press. Quoted by permission.

LIBRARY OF CONGRESS CATALOGING-IN-PUBLICATION DATA:
Ber, Victor.
Genos dikanikon : amateur and professional speech in the courtrooms of classical Athens /
Victor Bers.
    p. cm. -- (Hellenic studies ; 33)
 Includes bibliographical references and index.
 SBN 978-0-674-03203-3 (alk. paper)
1. Forensic orations--Greece--Athens--History. 2. Forensic oratory--History. 3. Rhetoric,
Ancient. I. Title. II. Series.
  KL4345.B47 2009
  347.38'5075--dc22

                                                                    2009016266

For my uncle, Harry Kagan

ACKNOWLEDGMENTS

I HAVE PRESENTED PARTS OF THIS BOOK at the École Normale Supérieure (Paris), Brown, Princeton, Harvard, Bryn Mawr, the 1998 meeting of the American Society of Legal Historians in Toronto, the New York Classical Club, Johns Hopkins, the Whitney Humanities Center at Yale, and the Bibliotheca Classica in St. Petersburg. My gratitude to those audiences, and also to Stephen Colvin, Martin Devecka, Adriaan Lanni, and Lene Rubinstein for advice on specific points. Joseph Roisman read the manuscript for the *Hellenica* series and gave me pages of *corrigenda et addenda* that made for a much better book. I thank Roberta Engleman for preparing the indices. Mary Bellino's editorial work repaired more mistakes than I care to remember.

When they were available at the time of writing, I use the translations of the Attic orators in the Oratory of Classical Greece series (general editor, Michael Gagarin), published by the University of Texas Press. Translations from Aristototle's *Rhetoric* by George A. Kennedy are taken from his *Aristotle, On Rhetoric: A Theory of Civic Discourse* (Oxford University Press, 1991). I am grateful to the University of Texas Press and Oxford University Press for permission to quote from these translations. Unless otherwise indicated, all other translations are my own.

CONTENTS

1

THE CHALLENGE OF COURT SPEECH

FEW ASPECTS OF CLASSICAL GREEK LITERATURE are as well preserved as the oratory of the lawcourts of classical Athens. Of the approximately 150 speeches composed by or attributed to the Attic orators who constitute the Canon, about two-thirds were written for real or imaginary forensic occasions. For some purposes we can also consult partly or entirely imaginary court speeches by Gorgias, Antisthenes, Alcidamas, Plato, and Xenophon. Attic oratory may be regarded as democracy's indispensable tool, but this tool was not thrown away once Athenian deliberative and judicial bodies lost their powers. If Quintilian is right, the introduction of imaginary forensic and deliberative rhetoric exercises, undoubtedly imitative of orators already recognized as good models, occurred almost immediately after the accession of Demetrius of Phaleron, who served the Macedonian kingdom as the plenipotentiary governor of Athens beginning in 317.[1] In any case, the study of Attic oratory was soon established as indispensable for all who aspired to a full share of Greek culture, whether they were members of the Greek-speaking upper classes or ambitious barbaroi.[2]

We find remarks on the quality of public speech as early as the *Iliad*, and by not later than the middle of the fifth century men were paid to teach other men to speak. It is impossible to say when judicial procedures were first thought to require a rhetoric different from those appropriate to political or ceremonial occasions, but by the fourth century the differentiation of rhetorical genres (*genê*) was well established (though there are some discrepancies in the number of genres and their names). The most

---

[1] *Institutio Oratoria* 2.4.41: . . . *fictas ad imitationem fori consiliorumque materias apud Graecos dicere circa Demetrium Phalerea institutum fere constat.* One might describe this as a revival of the practice embodied in Antiphon's *Tetralogies.*

[2] See Cribiore 2001, chap. 8, for specific examples of how rhetoric suffused not only elementary and higher education, but the lives of the elite once they left school. For the sinister historical consequences of a "rhetoricized mentality," see Rudich 1997.

authoritative statement, unsurprisingly, is Aristotle's in the *Rhetoric*. Working from a threefold distinction among speech occasions and their audiences, he concludes:

ἔστιν δ' ὁ μὲν περὶ τῶν μελλόντων κρίνων ὁ ἐκκλησιαστής, ὁ δὲ περὶ τῶν γεγενημένων ὁ δικαστής, ὁ δὲ περὶ τῆς δυνάμεως ὁ θεωρός, ὥστ' ἐξ ἀνάγκης ἂν εἴη τρία γένη τῶν λόγων τῶν ῥητορικῶν, συμβουλευτικόν, δικανικόν, ἐπιδεικτικόν.

A member of a democratic assembly is an example of one judging about future happenings, a juryman an example of one judging the past. A spectator is concerned with the ability [of the speaker].[3] Thus, there would necessarily be three genera [*genê*] of rhetorics; *symbouleutikon* ["deliberative"], *dikanikon* ["judicial"],[4] *epideiktikon* ["demonstrative"].

Rhetoric 1358b4–8 (trans. Kennedy 1991)

The variations are not significant; e.g. Anaximenes in the *Rhetorica ad Alexandrum*[5] uses the words *dêmêgorikon*, *epideiktikon*, and *dikanikon*. At *Phaedrus* 261a–b Plato speaks of rhetoric meant for law cases and "addresses to the people," using for the latter the term *dêmêgoria*, a word that suggests deliberative speech. But having quoted, or more likely written, a work supposedly in Lysias' epideictic style in the form of the *Erotikos* earlier in the dialogue (230e6–234c5), Plato cannot be said to be ignoring that branch of oratory.[6]

To Aristotle's disgust (*Rhetoric* 1354b19–27), writers on oratory were far more interested in the forensic than in the deliberative branch.[7] The large number of preserved forensic speeches is obviously advantageous to this study, but in one respect I must join Aristotle in deploring the relative paucity of preserved political speeches. In the Canon there are at most nineteen speeches written for the Athenian Assembly,[8] and with a few exceptions they

---

[3] This sentence has come under suspicion: see Kennedy 1991 ad loc.

[4] Kennedy's word, but I use 'forensic' throughout this monograph.

[5] The author is sometimes given as Pseudo-Aristotle.

[6] Cf. Plato *Sophist* 222c, where a "conversational" art forms a triad with forensic and political rhetoric.

[7] He was also disgusted by the audiences. Delivery is important "owing to the *mokhthêria* [incapacity, or even depravity] of the hearer" (*Rhetoric* 1404a8).

[8] Andocides 3 is probably a legitimate early example, but not the other candidates: see Hansen 1984:60 (= Hansen 1989:286), but cf. E. Harris 2000, who is certain the *De Pace* is a forgery.

are lamentably late. Compare speeches of Antiphon and Isaeus and you can see that forensic rhetoric was developing very rapidly indeed, but a direct comparison of roughly contemporary dicanic and symbouleutic speech is not possible until the middle of the fourth century.[9] Furthermore, a clean distinction between forensic and symbouleutic speech is often an illusion, particularly in dealing with court speeches written and delivered by leading politicians. The institutional status of a case might justify assignment of a speech to the *genos dikanikon*, though the significant issue is contemporary or retrospective political struggle: Aeschines 1 *Against Timarchus* and Demosthenes 18 *On the Crown* are notorious examples. The unavoidable consequence is that some of our evidence for stylistic features of the *genos dikanikon* is not as clear as we would like.[10]

Despite the good fortune that has preserved Attic court speeches in great profusion, along with a considerable body of relevant commentary and polemic,[11] the concrete reality and drama of the Attic courts was largely ignored by scholars until the mid-1980s.[12] Moreover, the overshadowing bulk of the preserved speeches – professional oratory composed by politicians for their own use, sometimes in court, and by *logographoi* (speechwriters) for other men to deliver – has created a sort of blind spot in the scholarship. With the exception of Isaeus, all the canonical orators took the podium in at least one forensic case,[13] but few litigants or their *synêgoroi* (co-speakers) were themselves *logographoi*. And in my view it is very likely that many litigants spoke in court with little or no professional help.[14] In this monograph I attempt to

[9] Comparisons within a single author's work are (or would be) of particular interest. For one example, see the discussion of Antiphon in chapter 3.

[10] On the other hand, epideictic oratory is so patently different that it is virtually invisible in this monograph.

[11] A few examples: Gorgias' *Helen*, Plato's *Phaedrus*, Aristotle's *Rhetoric*, and Dionysius of Halicarnassus in his essays on individual orators.

[12] Not, of course, entirely. Legal issues, largely treated from the perspective of the dominant European legal traditions, are prominent in the anthropologically informed work of Glotz and Gernet; Bonner, Gertrude Smith, and Dorjahn did important work on the analysis of procedure and some aspects of the "lower" speechmaking. As the title shows, Lavency 1964, an excellent piece of work, is explicitly about the professionals.

[13] I am assuming that Isocrates spoke for himself at the actual *diadikasia* whose outcome provides the pretext for his imaginary speech, the *Antidosis*. Apollodorus, sometimes called the Eleventh Attic Orator, also spoke in court.

[14] Although skeptics (e.g. Usher 1976) seem to be in the majority, I believe that Dover (1968b) has demonstrated the great probability that even in the preserved speeches there may be a mixture of amateur "client" and professional "consultant." If Dover (1968b:150f.) had no other evidence to adduce than Aristophanes *Knights* 347–350, his argument would be hard to dismiss. For the incidence of amateur speech in the courts, see my discussion in chapter 2.

show that many features of Athenian court speech in the deluxe form we know from the preserved speeches were fashioned to avoid the failings of amateur speech. Coining a Latin word, I call those defects *evitanda*, things to avoid.

If all we knew of the language of the Athenian lawcourts was what Aristotle says in the third book of the *Rhetoric*, we might suppose that the stylistic requirements in composition were minimal:

> δεῖ δὲ μὴ λεληθέναι ὅτι ἄλλη ἑκάστῳ γένει ἁρμόττει λέξις. οὐ γὰρ ἡ αὐτὴ γραφικὴ καὶ ἀγωνιστική, οὐδὲ δημηγορικὴ καὶ δικανική. ἄμφω δὲ ἀνάγκη εἰδέναι· τὸ μὲν γάρ ἐστιν ἑλληνίζειν ἐπίστασθαι ...

> One should not forget that a different *lexis* is appropriate for each genus [of rhetoric]. For the written and agonistic [style] are not the same; nor are the demegoric [deliberative] and the dicanic [judicial]; and it is necessary to know both. [Debate] consists of knowing how to speak good Greek.

> *Rhetoric* 1413b6 (trans. Kennedy 1991)[15]

Similarly, Isocrates makes dicanic speech a sort of ostensible "non-style." He says that among the sorts of discourses that he did *not* write as a young man were "those that when spoken seem simple and unadorned, such as people skillful in courts teach the young to practice if they want to have the advantage in litigation" (*Panathenaicus* 1).[16] Isocrates does at least allow the possibility that the simplicity of the spoken form conceals some artifice, but some ten years earlier in the *Panegyricus* (4.11) he enunciated a more trenchant opinion:

> [S]ome criticize speeches that are beyond ordinary citizens [*idiôtai*] and are too carefully composed. They have so misjudged things that they analyze elaborate speeches by comparing them to those written for trials about private contracts, as if the two types must be

---

[15] One point may require clarification: the component of rhetoric Kennedy identifies as "debate" takes in both symbouleutic (political) and dicanic (forensic) oratory. Cf. *Rhetoric* 1407a19–b25, where Aristotle includes among the constituents of "speaking good Greek" the correct use of connective particles, the use of specific words rather than circumlocutions, and the avoidance of unintentional ambiguity in various forms, e.g. phraseology difficult for the hearer to properly segment.

[16] τοὺς ἁπλῶς δοκοῦντας εἰρῆσθαι καὶ μηδεμιᾶς κομψότητος μετέχοντας, οὓς οἱ δεινοὶ περὶ τοὺς ἀγῶνας παραινοῦσι τοῖς νεωτέροις μελετᾶν, εἴπερ βούλονται πλέον ἔχειν τῶν ἀντιδίκων.

similar, when in fact one is plain [aphelôs],[17] and the other is demonstrative [epideiktikôs], or as if they themselves observe the middle course while those who know how to speak precisely cannot speak simply.[18]

Still, an idiôtês needing to speak in court might not see his task as one for which he commanded the necessary skills, even if Isocrates thought it required nothing but a "plain" style.

Nowhere does Aristotle suggest that the language of the Athenian courts deviated in lexicon or phraseology from the Attic speech that could be heard just outside the courtrooms when logographoi were chatting informally, say in the perfume, shoemaker, and barber shops nearest the Agora mentioned by the speaker at Lysias 24.20. Our knowledge of that everyday or "routine" Attic is imperfectly cobbled together, mostly from Old Comedy, by stripping away as best we can the paratragedy and other manifestly comic uses of language and the effects of versification. Assuming we have some confidence in our ability to determine certain features of routine Attic, we can compare that sort of language to dicanic speech. What we find is that there are deviations between routine and dicanic speech in lexicon, phraseology, and, to a much lesser extent, syntax; some of these deviations are blatant, others remarkably subtle. A number are examined in the chapters that follow, but I suspect that others are waiting to be discovered. One of my goals is to offer an economical explanation for these discrepancies in linguistic usage.

I argue in this monograph (1) that the professional component of the genos dikanikon represents only a portion of the speechmaking that went on in the Athenian courts; (2) that many men constrained to rely entirely or mainly on their own resources also spoke in court; (3) that their speech in court resembled routine speech in a number of ways, and that in these they differ from professional speech; (4) that professional speech was crafted to avoid certain features of amateur speech that seemed to cause a speaker's failure, features I call evitanda, in particular those that manifested excessive emotion when it was in his interest to appear unafraid and unperturbed. In a short appendix I discuss the shortcomings, as I see it, of the currently prevailing

---

[17] See Papillon's note for a defense of the emendation he translates in preference to the transmitted reading.

[18] καίτοι τινὲς ἐπιτιμῶσι τῶν λόγων τοῖς ὑπὲρ τοὺς ἰδιώτας ἔχουσι καὶ λίαν ἀπηκριβωμένοις, καὶ τοσοῦτον διημαρτήκασιν ὥστε τοὺς πρὸς ὑπερβολὴν πεποιημένους πρὸς τοὺς ἀγῶνας τοὺς περὶ τῶν ἰδίων συμβολαίων σκοποῦσιν, ὥσπερ ὁμοίως δέον ἀμφοτέρους ἔχειν, ἀλλ' οὐ τοὺς μὲν ἀφελῶς, τοὺς δ' ἐπιδεικτικῶς, ἢ σφᾶς μὲν διορῶντας τὰς μετριότητας, τὸν δ' ἀκριβῶς ἐπιστάμενον λέγειν ἁπλῶς οὐκ ἂν δυνάμενον εἰπεῖν.

explanation of professional dicanic speech as formal (rather than colloquial), a continuation of a preference for restraint in public speech at Athens or, more broadly, earlier written prose.

2

AMATEUR LITIGANTS, AMATEUR SPEAKERS

The *idiôtês* on His Own

I OFTEN SAID THAT A LITIGANT in an Athenian court was required to speak for himself,[1] though the evidence for an actual law making such a stipulation is very weak indeed: a single remark in a second-century AD work, Quintilian's *Institutio Oratoria* (2.15.30).[2] Still, even if litigants always delivered at least part of their pleadings in their own voices, there is no doubt whatever that many yielded their position on the *bêma* to *sunêgoroi* (co-speakers) and, more important, that our knowledge of court speech is necessarily drawn almost entirely from the preserved speeches of the ten *logographoi* (speechwriters) of the Canon of Attic Orators and Apollodorus (the "Eleventh Attic Orator"; see Trevett 1992). The canonical status of these orators is to blame, as I see it, for a blind spot that has led scholars to regard the preserved speeches as a reliable sample of how the generality of Athenians spoke in court. We see this in Dover's magnificent analysis of forensic style: "It is . . . demonstrable that conformity of language to litigant falls within certain boundaries, and that in the Lysian period a certain distance between forensic language and colloquial language was maintained, no matter how simple and plain-spoken the persona of the litigant might be" (Dover 1968b:83). Dover did establish that discrepancy in his specimen texts (Dover 1968b:83–86). His results are of great significance. But for his purposes, colloquial language was represented

---

[1] To cite a by now old example, the first page (v) of Bonner 1927: "The law required every man to plead his own case in court"; and a recent one: "each prosecutor and each defendant had to speak for himself" (Goldhill 2002:62). Kennedy 1998:219 adds an even more doubtful "expectation" pertaining to symbouleutic (political) speech: "Male citizens were expected to speak in the political assembly and were required to speak on their own behalf in prosecution and defense in the courts of law."

[2] For a brief survey of opinion on the matter, see Rubinstein 2000:14.

by comic narrative; he makes no mention of litigants who could not speak in court in the language of the *logographoi*.[3]

A portion of my general argument on the nature of unskilled dicanic speech is built from traces, some direct, some inferred, of speeches poorly prepared and poorly executed. Even a professional *logographos* writing and delivering his own speech must have stumbled from time to time, but my general hypothesis is that certain *evitanda* (things that should be avoided) were characteristic of court speech performed by men forced by circumstance to rely exclusively on themselves or on friends and relatives no more adept at forensic speaking than themselves. For the sake of brevity, I usually refer to a man in this category as an *idiôtês* (plural *idiôtai*), a word that in general denotes men with little or no training and practice in a specific activity;[4] in Athens the term was a few times used of volunteer prosecutors, but far more often in a negative sense of individuals who were not *rhêtores* (speakers), *politeuomenoi* (men regularly involved in politics), or "skilled in speaking or maneuvering" (see Rubinstein 1998). But it cannot be taken for granted that enough men who lacked professional skill of their own and did not enjoy a professional's assistance actually spoke – and spoke poorly – in Athenian courts that their failures can serve as the foil against which to inspect certain qualities of professional speech. Or to put it another way, we must ask to what extent the one hundred or so forensic speeches in our corpus are *unrepresentative* of actual court speech. Were there opportunities for Athenians to witness or hear about speeches that went awry in ways that *logographoi* would identify and avoid in their own work?

Idiôtai Too Poor to Pay a *logographos*?

We meet a few tantalizing references to a speaker's economic status. At Demosthenes 44.3–4 *Against Leochares* the speaker describes himself and his father as poor (*penês*; see the discussion of *Birds* 1430–36 later in this chapter), adding that his father works as a sort of town crier or messenger, an occupation that allows him no free time to "fuss with business." Still, the case involves an estate large enough to make buying a professional speech at least a reasonable gamble. The entire point of Lysias 24 is to persuade the *Boulê*

---

[3] To be sure, Dover's method has the advantage of working directly from preserved texts; what I attempt is of course more speculative.

[4] A subset of the *idiôtai* would be the country types mentioned by Aristotle *Rhetoric* 1408a9: "A rustic and an educated person would not say the same thing nor [say it] in the same way" (trans. Kennedy 1991).

that the speaker is entitled, by virtue of a crippling disability that has exacerbated his poverty, to a daily payment from the state of one obol, a very small sum indeed. Some scholars (e.g. Usher 1999:106–110) cannot believe that a man as poor as he claims to be could afford to buy a speech from a *logographos*, and that the levity the speaker exhibits is impossibly cheeky. In their view, the speech is a bagatelle, the client nonexistent. Todd (2000:253–254), who is rightly agnostic on the issue, points to a number of possible explanations for a poor man getting professional help, including the chance "that the orator (whether Lysias or somebody else) might be prepared to reduce or waive his fees in the light of a personal connection with the speaker."[5]

The prosecutor in Isocrates 20.19 talks as if from and for the proletariat:

καὶ μηδεὶς ὑμῶν, εἰς τοῦτ' ἀποβλέψας ὅτι πένης εἰμὶ καὶ τοῦ πλήθους εἷς, ἀξιούτω τοῦ τιμήματος ἀφαιρεῖν. οὐ γὰρ δίκαιον ἐλάττους ποιεῖσθαι τὰς τιμωρίας ὑπὲρ τῶν ἀδόξων ἢ τῶν διωνομασμένων, οὐδὲ χείρους ἡγεῖσθαι τοὺς πενομένους ἢ τοὺς πολλὰ κεκτημένους. ὑμᾶς γὰρ ἂν αὐτοὺς ἀτιμάζοιτ' εἰ τοιαῦτα γιγνώσκοιτε περὶ τῶν πολιτῶν.

Let not even one of you think it right to reduce the award because you have observed that I am poor, one of the many. It is unjust to make the penalty less for little-known victims than those who have much. You would be dishonoring yourselves if you thought such things about citizens.

Can we believe his self-description as "poor, one of the many"? David Mirhady, the translator, remarks that "most of the judges would also have been relatively poor." That fact alone might taint the argument for justice for the poor because the speaker appeals to the jury as if they were better off, a piece of dishonest flattery. The very brevity of the speech, at least as we have it – only a few pages – might be evidence for the speaker's poverty, but we must beware of begging the larger question by assuming that Isocrates' fee was too high for a poor man.

The following discussion will, of necessity, simplify the issue by casting it as a dichotomy: skilled logographic speech versus unskilled amateur work. If it were not impossibly cumbrous, however, I would repeatedly invoke (and expand on) Dover (1968b: chap. 8) by calling attention to a continuum: At

---

[5] For a survey of orators' strategies in countering prejudice against the rich see Ober 1989, chap. 5, esp. 220–226.

the high end, a *logographos* composing and delivering a speech himself; next would follow a client willing and able to pay for a complete speech and some coaching in the delivery; then a litigant who could read well enough to learn from written speeches, whether model speeches[6] or ones actually delivered, or if rich enough to mingle with experienced men, to ask their advice;[7] a self-reliant litigant who had learned by observation, e.g. as a spectator (see Lanni 1997); a man buying in the "bargain basement," perhaps getting just a sketch of a speech and a few worked-out paragraphs, and then doing some rehearsing. At the extreme low end, we would find a functional illiterate making an unrehearsed, truly spontaneous speech – an extremity, it must be remembered, that Dover does not spell out. Damaging mistakes would presumably cluster toward the end of this spectrum, but καὶ Ὅμηρος ἔνευσε (the proverbial "even Homer nods"), and even a Lysias or an Aeschines could make a mistake others would notice and resolve not to repeat.

We would have a much better handle on this matter if speakers were forthcoming, precise, and credible about their economic status and about the preparation of their speeches,[8] but not one comes within a *stadion*'s length of such candor. Consequently, we need to look outside the *genos dikanikon* in the form it has reached us.

Poor Men in Court?

Although many specific Athenians can be identified as members of the liturgic class, the richest in the city, overall distribution of wealth in classical Athens is not known with any precision. The size of the next richest group, not subject to liturgies but only to payment of the *eisphora*, sometimes called the "leisure class," is controversial.[9] But if the curve, virtually an L, presented by Davies 1981 (graph opposite 36) is even roughly accurate, the citizen population was predominantly quite poor, and the number of men whose "gross wealth" exceeded a talent very small. Was the average – that is to say, poor – Athenian at all likely to have spoken in court? And if he was, did he have professional help?

---

[6] Cooper 2007:206 with n15 refers to the works of Anaxagoras selling at one drachma that Plato has Socrates mention at *Apology* 25d, and remarks that "presumably works on rhetoric came equally cheap." I think that Plato is engaging in mockery, not accurate reportage, and that full speeches (if they were available in 399) would have cost far more.

[7] Hawhee 2004:13 and chaps. 5 and 6 speculates on the gymnasium as a locus for citizen training.

[8] Plato's Socrates obviously does not count as an exception; even the historical Socrates, reported verbatim, would be a sui generis litigant.

[9] For a compact review of this question see Hansen 1990.

Several scholars who have written on the subject have tended to the opinion that poorer men were very rarely heard in court. In *Mass and Elite in Democratic Athens*, Ober remarks, "The Athenians had a reputation for being an especially litigious folk (cf. Aristophanes, *Wasps*, *Clouds*), but we do not know how common it was for an average Athenian to find himself involved in a lawsuit" (1989:112–113). The general argument of Ober's book, however, presents a picture of the courts as an arena in which rich men were the contestants and poorer men the judges.[10] Christ attacks the question head-on and is less agnostic than Ober: "To be sure, the surviving record may give a skewed impression of the sociology of Athenian litigation, since the forensic speeches that constitute the bulk of the ancient evidence were composed for well-off litigants. Nonetheless, it is probable that elite Athenians, that is, the top 5 to 10 percent of citizens by wealth, constituted a 'litigating class' that was disproportionately active in the courts" (1998:32–33). His conclusion arises from three arguments: (1) "The circumstances of wealthy men increased the likelihood of their engaging in litigation." The rich had property worth fighting over, say in an inheritance suit, or they might be "victims of false suits." They were far more likely to be active in the city's political life, and therefore more vulnerable to legal action, and they were also subject to liturgical service and the legal troubles that came with it. (2) "The wealthy were in a much better position than average citizens to initiate and pursue suits. . . . They could afford to study oratory in anticipation of litigation, to purchase speeches from logographers for use at trial." (3) "Athenian legal institutions privileged legal conflicts among the rich and powerful in several ways": cases involving less than ten drachmas were decided by deme judges; longer sessions were allotted for trials arising from disputes in which large sums were at stake; and *graphai*, the category of action more likely to involve rich citizens, got a whole day in court (Christ 1998:33).

These are all substantial points, but in my view not strong enough to show that the unaided *idiôtês* was virtually invisible – or perhaps better, inaudible – in the Athenian courts. I side with Rhodes (1998:145), who notes that "there were enough private suits for the Forty to decide those for under ten drachmae and for all men in their last year on the army registers to be used as arbitrators to decide those for over ten drachmae." He goes on to conjecture

---

[10] Roisman (2005:118) offers no opinion on the subject, merely stating the undeniable fact that "[m]ost of the claimants and defendants featured in the orations came from the social and financial elite."

that the *idiôtês* was not a rarity among litigators:[11] "It looks as if the Athenians' reputation for litigiousness was not generated only by the elite, but a significant number of Athenians pursued quarrels by judicial means significantly often. I should guess that in the law-courts as in the Assembly the man who was a mere voter on one day might well be an active participant on another."

Consider first the ten-drachma rule. The source is the *Constitution of the Athenians* attributed to Aristotle (53.1–2):

κληροῦσι δὲ καὶ τοὺς τετταράκοντα, τέτταρας ἐκ τῆς φυλῆς ἑκάστης, πρὸς οὓς τὰς ἄλλας δίκας λαγχάνουσιν. οἳ πρότερον μὲν ἦσαν τριάκοντα καὶ κατὰ δήμους περιιόντες ἐδίκαζον, μετὰ δὲ τὴν ἐπὶ τῶν τριάκοντα ὀλιγαρχίαν τετταράκοντα γεγόνασιν. καὶ τὰ μὲν μέχρι δέκα δραχμῶν αὐτοτελεῖς εἰσι δ[ικά]ζε[ι]ν

The Forty, four appointed by lot from each tribe, are the officials from whom the plaintiffs obtain a hearing in the other private suits. Earlier they were thirty in number, and used to go round the demes trying cases, but since the oligarchy of the Thirty there have been forty of them. Cases up to ten drachmae they have absolute authority to decide, cases above this assessment they hand over to the arbitrators.

(Trans. P. J. Rhodes)

This upper limit for compulsory adjudication of a case by a deme judge was very low. The most often cited record of wages, the Erechtheum accounts of the last decade of the fifth century, show that a laborer would earn ten drachmas in seven to ten days (*IG* I² 373–374). We might compare the current typical dollar limits of $2,500 to $5,000 in American small claims court, the lowest reach of the system. These are amounts a blue-collar worker might earn in one to three months.[12] Some eighty years after the Erechtheum accounts, not long after the terminus post quem of the *Constitution of the Athenians*, skilled workers at Eleusis would earn ten drachmas in as few as four days (*IG* II–III² 1672–1673). That service as an arbitrator was obligatory for citizens once they reached their fifty-ninth birthday (*Constitution of the Athenians* 53.4) suggests that the city needed to make provision for a large number of men seeking

---

[11] An easy inference from the severe penalties assessed against men who evade this service (Aristotle *Constitution of the Athenians* 53.5).

[12] In a few jurisdictions, however, limits are far higher; see www.nolo.com/lawcenter/ency/article.cfm/objectID/ADF1FA1B-C67D-4B95-AD615532C3AE0862.

recourse to the legal system, whether by arbitration or jury trial. At some point the city excluded the ephebes, at least some of whom must have come from families of *idiôtai*, from participation in *dikai*, whether as prosecutors or defendants (*Constitution of the Athenians* 42.5).[13] Finally, it is important to keep in mind that a potential litigant might descend from a rich family or have rich descendants of his own, yet have very little property himself.[14]

Furthermore, we should not assume that there is a tight connection between a man's fitness to cope with litigation and his need to do so. Any lawyer serving destitute clients in contemporary America knows this melancholy situation very well. The poor could sometimes be attacked to settle a personal grievance, whether justified or not, or be milked of the little they had by pitiless opportunists adept at manipulating the legal system. And it should go without saying that a poor man could be accused, whether justly or not, of a serious crime of violence and subject to summary arrest (*apagôgê*). Unless he admitted to guilt and accepted immediate execution, he would need to speak at his trial.[15] Would a man who earned as little as these laborers did think it worthwhile or even possible to pay for assistance? Isocrates asserts that Athens was very well stocked with *logographoi*,[16] but even if that was true, he does not speak about the cost of their services.

As early as the *Clouds* (the first version was performed in 423) there is evidence that one did have to pay for help in coping with litigation. Deluxe rhetorical training might involve study with a sophist, and sophists, as Dover puts it, "did not teach for nothing" (Dover 1968a:xxxix; cf. Xenophon *Memorabilia* 1.6). Aristophanes' Strepsiades, explaining to his son that he might go to a *phrontistêrion* (a building for mental reflection – the word is nicely captured by 'reflectory')[17] to learn from Socrates and his gang the means to throw off his creditors, certainly expects to pay for this knowledge:

---

[13] Excepting only inheritance cases. Admittedly, the text gives a motive other than relieving court congestion: καὶ δίκην οὔτε διδόασιν οὔτε λαμβάνουσιν, ἵνα μὴ πρό[φ]ασις ᾖ τ[ο]ῦ ἀπιέναι.

[14] See Davies 1981, chap. 5, on the instability of fortune. He cites Demosthenes 42.4: τὸ διευτυχεῖν συνεχῶς τῇ οὐσίᾳ οὐ πολλοῖς τῶν πολιτῶν διαμένειν εἴθισται (87; see also Xenophon *Memorabilia* 2.8.1–6 [Eutheros]). The speaker of Demosthenes 57 says that his father, whom he describes as poor (*penês*), had to defend his Athenian citizenship before assemblies of his deme and phratry, and that he himself is sometimes reviled for his poverty (*penia*).

[15] Unless, that is, there was no requirement that a defendant speak in his own defense and he could place the entire burden on *synêgoroi* (see the opening of this section).

[16] *Antidosis* 41: "... that those who compose speeches for others who have cases in the lawcourts are legion is apparent to everyone."

[17] I heard "reflectory" first from my teacher Benedict Einarson, but do not know whether this was his own fine invention.

ψυχῶν σοφῶν τοῦτ' ἐστὶ φροντιστήριον.
ἐνταῦθ' ἐνοικοῦσ' ἄνδρες οἳ τὸν οὐρανὸν
λέγοντες ἀναπείθουσιν ὡς ἔστιν πνιγεύς,
κἄστιν περὶ ἡμᾶς οὗτος, ἡμεῖς δ' ἄνθρακες.
οὗτοι διδάσκουσ', ἀργύριον ἤν τις διδῷ,
λέγοντα νικᾶν καὶ δίκαια κἄδικα.

This is the "reflectory" of shrewd minds. Dwelling within are men
who say that the firmament is a cauldron lid that surrounds us, and
we are the charcoal. These men teach tuition-paying customers to
win by giving speeches – both just and unjust.

Clouds 94–99

In a fragment of what at least purports to be Antiphon's celebrated
speech in his own defense for involvement with the oligarchy of the Four
Hundred, he mentions, in order to dismiss as improbable, the charge that he
profited from law cases:

ἀλλὰ μὲν δὴ λέγουσιν οἱ κατήγοροι ὡς συνέγραφόν τε δίκας ἄλλοις
καὶ ὡς ἐκέρδαινον ἀπὸ τούτου. οὐκοῦν ἐν μὲν τῆι ὀλιγαρχίαι οὐκ ἂν
ἦν μοι τοῦτο, ἐν τῆι δημοκρατίαι πάλαι ὁ κρατῶν εἰμι ἐγώ εἰδὼς τοῦ
λέγειν, ἐν μὲν τῆι ὀλιγαρχίαι οὐδενὸς ἔμελλον ἄξιος ἔσεσθαι, ἐν δὲ
τῆι δημοκρατίαι πολλοῦ;

My accusers say that I used to compose speeches for others
to deliver in court, and that I profited from this. But under an
oligarchy I would not be able to do this, whereas under a democracy I have long been the one with power because of my skill with
words. I would be worthless in an oligarchy but very valuable in
a democracy.

Antiphon fr. 1.10–15 Gagarin

This suggests a widespread familiarity with at least the imputation of
speechwriters' venality; together with jokes and other reports on the same
theme, it must reflect, at the very least, a common opinion.[18] Regrettably, we

---

[18] See Lavency 1964:59 with n2. Of course, no opinion is necessarily true just because it is
common. In the early years of the Iraqi war, a substantial number of Americans, and an even
greater portion of American troops in Iraq, believed that Saddam Hussein was complicit in the
terror actions of September 11, 2001.

have no solid evidence regarding what one had to pay for a logographer's help.[19] Socrates is a special case, an ascetic (*Clouds* 103) often invited to dine in rich men's houses, but the famous sophists are portrayed as living very well indeed, if we can trust the many relevant Platonic texts. The unspoken premise of Antiphon's remark, however, is that he was drawing an income from his speechwriting substantial enough to make it implausible for him to participate in a coup d'état to bring down the democracy. Jokes in fourth-century comedy also make no sense if the famous speechwriters were working for peanuts, rather to satisfy luxurious tastes (Timocles fr. 4 K-A). It seems close to certain that the better *logographoi*, the men whose work was commercially viable in the book trade, charged far more than those too poor to be assigned liturgies or to pay *eisphora* could (or would) choose to pay.

At Demosthenes 22.25–29 *Against Androtion* the speaker stresses, and rather exaggerates (Carey 1998), the multiplicity of procedures available under Athenian law. He refers to Athenians who are bold and capable of speaking or who are not adept (§25, δυνατοῖς λέγειν vs. ἰδίωτας). He also speaks of the monetary risks of various actions. This makes sense only if the jury thinks it possible that poor men, untrained in public speaking, might sometimes find themselves wishing or needing to participate as agents in prosecution or defense.

There is plentiful evidence from the comic stage. If we had no other proof of the prominence of lawcourts in Athenian life, we might not be sure whether the many jokes about litigiousness were simply drawing on a comic *topos*, an urban myth, as it were.[20] But of course there is abundance of evidence for an extremely active judicial apparatus in texts far from the comic stage and in material remains. That said, can we deduce anything from comedy about the social and economic status of litigants?

Several of the most famous jokes tell us little more than that courts forever in session were a notorious feature at Athens:

[Μαθητής] αὕτη δέ σοι γῆς περίοδος πάσης. ὁρᾷς; αἵδε μὲν Ἀθῆναι.

[Στρεψιάδης] τί σὺ λέγεις; οὐ πείθομαι,ἐπεὶ δικαστὰς οὐχ ὁρῶ καθημένους.

---

[19] When first published, the text appeared to allude to a 20 percent fee, but this was a misreading of the papyrus by the editor: see Dover 1968b:157–158.

[20] The supposedly numerous "welfare queens" living luxuriously on public funds come to mind as another example of such a myth.

Student: This is a map of the word. See? Here is Athens.

Strepsiades: What do you mean? I don't believe it, because I don't see jurymen at work.

Clouds 206–208

And in Aristophanes' *Peace* (505), Hermes charges the Athenians with doing nothing but adjudicating court cases: οὐδὲν γὰρ ἄλλο δρᾶτε πλὴν δικάζετε ("You do nothing but decide cases"). At *Wasps* 87–90, a similar description applies to Philocleon, the jury-service addict:

φράσω γὰρ ἤδη τὴν νόσον τοῦ δεσπότου.
φιληλιαστής ἐστιν ὡς οὐδεὶς ἀνήρ·
ἐρᾷ τε τούτου τοῦ δικάζειν, καὶ στένει
ἢν μὴ 'πὶ τοῦ πρώτου καθίζηται ξύλου.

I'll tell you our master's disease: he's a lover of the lawcourt, like no one else. He's passionate for this business of judging, and he moans if he doesn't sit on the front-row bench.

So far we have descriptions not of litigants, but of jurors. To the extent that we can rely on the documentary value of Aristophanes' jokes, we have reason to believe that the courts were known to have been busy places and that many Athenians sat on jury panels. At Aristophanes *Birds* 39–41, however, the Athenians are most probably litigants, since they are described as vocalizing:

οἱ μὲν γὰρ οὖν τέττιγες ἕνα μῆν' ἢ δύο
ἐπὶ τῶν κραδῶν ᾄδουσ', Ἀθηναῖοι δ' ἀεὶ
ἐπὶ τῶν δικῶν ᾄδουσι πάντα τὸν βίον.

The cicadas sit on their boughs and sing a month or two, whereas the Athenians sit on their law cases forever and sing their whole life through.[21]

Philocleon's sadism, which is depicted as aimed solely at defendants, and his uncertain economic standing make it hard to be sure whether Aristophanes was expecting his audience to recognize a typical litigant in Philocleon's vignettes. The defendant whom Philocleon quotes at 556–557

---

[21] The insects' more or less continuous singing more closely resembles speech per se than the intermittent and polyphonic jurors' *thorubos*.

is poor enough to confess what sounds like petty larceny in the discharge of a magistracy or when buying provisions on campaign:

"οἴκτιρόν μ', ὦ πάτερ, αἰτοῦμαί σ', εἰ καὐτὸς πώποθ' ὑφείλου
ἀρχὴν ἄρξας ἢ 'πὶ στρατιᾶς τοῖς ξυσσίτοις ἀγοράζων."

"Pity me, father, I beg you, if you yourself ever swiped something while holding office, or, when on campaign, buying provisions for your messmates."

But the next defendant in Philocleon's description (564–565) is apparently putting on a false show of poverty:

οἱ μέν γ' ἀποκλάονται πενίαν αὑτῶν, καὶ προστιθέασιν κακὰ πρὸς
τοῖς οὖσιν, ἕως ἂν ἰὼν ἀνισώσῃ τοῖσιν ἐμοῖσιν·

Some of them wail about their poverty, and pile troubles on the ones they really have, until they equal my troubles.

We hear of several additional devices some other defendants (οἱ δέ bis) employ in an attempt to win pity from the jurors, and then Philocleon concludes with a line (575) suggesting that these litigants, at least, have some measure of wealth: ἆρ' οὐ μεγάλη τοῦτ' ἔστ' ἀρχὴ καὶ τοῦ πλούτου καταχήνη; ("Isn't this a powerful office, the snubbing of wealth?").

Aristophanes assigns Philocleon several motives for jury service, including the satisfaction of his sadism and other more or less base desires, but the chief attraction is financial, the three-obol fee (605–610) that he brings home to a family that adores him for it; accordingly, he is undone by his son's demonstration that the jurors are in fact receiving far less than their fair share (660–695). The plot practically demands that the litigants be portrayed as at least richer than the jurors;[22] his son places him among a large group whom unscrupulous politicians "wish to be poor." But there are passages in the *Wasps* suggesting that poorer men might find themselves not only compelled to appear in court, but even taking the initiative in a legal action. Rather late in the play (1094–1097) the elderly chorus of jurors, who had earlier been presented as far from well off (251–253; 300–302), contrast their current interest in doing well in court with their youthful devotion as younger men to military exploits:

[22] Philocleon presents himself as a poor man (1132–1133, 1170, 1188–1189), but his son is evidently fairly well off: see MacDowell ad *Wasps* 10. On the economic status of the jurors see Markle 1985.

οὐ γὰρ ἦν ἡμῖν ὅπως
ῥῆσιν εὖ λέξειν ἐμέλλο-
μεν τότ' οὐδὲ
συκοφαντήσειν τινὰ
φροντίς, ἀλλ' ὅστις ἐρέτης ἔσοιτ' ἄριστος.

You see, then we didn't give a thought to making a good speech or maliciously going after someone in the courts, but to who would be the best rower.

The first element, how to speak well, might pertain to defense or a deliberative speech in the Assembly, but the second is frankly prosecutorial, attacking a man in a legal action, probably without justification. Soon after (1205–1207), Philocleon brags of his own successful prosecution of a famous athlete for verbal abuse:

ἐγῷδα τοίνυν τό γε νεανικώτατον·
ὅτε τὸν δρομέα Φάυλλον ὢν βούπαις ἔτι
εἷλον διώκων λοιδορίας ψήφοιν δυοῖν.

I know the coolest thing was when I was still a *huge* kid and prosecuted Phayllos the runner for insulting language, and won my case by a two-vote margin.

The "reformed" and rejuvenated Philocleon behaves like a rank hooligan. He has abandoned jury service, but around him people continue to look to the courts for redress, or at least pretend that they will. Speaking for a group whom Philocleon has just treated roughly, a man threatens him with legal action (1332–1334), presumably for αἰκία (assault) or ὕβρις (assault that dimishes the victim's honor):

ἦ μὴν σὺ δώσεις αὔριον τούτων δίκην
ἡμῖν ἅπασιν, κεἰ σφόδρ' εἶ νεανίας.

I swear you'll answer for this in court, for all of us, even if you *are* a young fellow.

Soon after (1415–1418), Bdelycleon warns his father that a second assault victim is coming after him, accompanied by a witness.[23] This time the potential prosecutor names the specific offense, ὕβρις.

---

[23] See MacDowell ad loc. for the erroneous identification of this man as Euripides in two manuscripts.

[Βδελυκλέων] ὁδί τις ἕτερος, ὡς ἔοικεν, ἔρχεται
καλούμενός σε· τόν γέ τοι κλητῆρ' ἔχει.

[Κατήγορος] οἴμοι κακοδαίμων. προσκαλοῦμαί σ', ὦ γέρον,
ὕβρεως.

Bdelycleon: Here's another guy coming to summon you; he does at
least have a witness.

Prosecutor: Oh, my awful luck! I summon you, old man, for assault.

Bdelycleon offers to settle, but his father goes him one better, confessing his
guilt, proposing (absurdly) to take it on himself to determine the amount
of damages, and offering his friendship to boot. The victim accepts, out of
reluctance to get involved in legal action (1426):

[Κατήγορος] σὺ λέγε. δικῶν γὰρ οὐ δέομ' οὐδὲ πραγμάτων.

Prosecutor: You say – how much to settle? I don't want lawsuits
or trouble.

Legal action is, then, at least one of the likely outcomes. Within a few lines,
Philocleon again strikes the victim and launches into his second cautionary
tale. The action, set in Philocleon's private court, calls for court performances
by kitchen implements and dogs; likewise, this *exemplum* tells of a jar seeking
redress through legal action (1435–1441). These jokes about inanimate objects
as participants in litigation rely on a reductio ad absurdum: not just anyone,
but any thing, could find himself/itself in court and required to speak. This
comic premise would, I think, have been unworkable if elite litigants were
practically the only ones Athenians could see contending in the courts.

The episode also includes the appearance of Myrtia the bread-seller, who
as a woman would of course not be permitted to represent herself in legal
proceedings, threatening to prosecute Philocleon for knocking her wares to
the ground. Though a citizen, she is at the low end of the economic ladder.
Along with her is a member of the elite, the often-satirized Chaerephon,
whom she identifies as a witness of Philocleon's offense. But as Chaerephon
is involved only because he happened to be present, we cannot doubt that
the de facto potential litigant is Myrtia herself, a woman poor enough to be
selling bread.

Comedy does not, unfortunately, supply clear evidence as to the
economic class of the sycophants (malicious prosecutors; cf. Demosthenes *On
the Crown* 242), a group whose occupation was disparaged in forensic oratory

perhaps as early as Antiphon.[24] True, a passage like the colloquy between Peisetaerus and the Sycophant at *Birds* 1430–1436 suggests that the practice of συκοφαντία aims at providing an income at least this particular sycophant would otherwise earn by honest physical toil, the sort of work a πένης (poor, but basically self-sufficient), not a πλούσιος (rich, sometimes with the nuance "filthy rich") would perform:

[Πεισέταιρος] τουτὶ γὰρ ἐργάζει σὺ τοὔργον; Εἰπέ μοι,
νεανίας ὢν συκοφαντεῖς τοὺς ξένους;

[Συκοφάντης] τί γὰρ πάθω; Σκάπτειν γὰρ οὐκ ἐπίσταμαι.

[Πεισέταιρος] ἀλλ᾽ ἔστιν ἕτερα νὴ Δί᾽ ἔργα σώφρονα,
ἀφ᾽ ὧν διαζῆν ἄνδρα χρῆν τοσουτονὶ
ἐκ τοῦ δικαίου μᾶλλον ἢ δικορραφεῖν.

Peisetaerus: *This* is your job? Tell me, young man that you are: you hound foreigners in the courts?

Sycophant: Damn straight I do. I don't know how to dig.

Peisetaerus: But by Zeus, there *are* other respectable jobs from which you could be making a living – a man your size – honestly, instead of stitching together lawsuits.

As the types seeking a place in Cloudcuckooland are all hoping for some advantage, it would be difficult for Aristophanes to insert into the parade a man whose riches were already secure. Similarly, it would be inconvenient for Aristophanes' plot to portray the Sycophant in *Wealth* (848–958) as a member of the city's propertied class, enjoying a steady income.

In any case, a voluntary participant in court argument, whether we regard him as a malicious opportunist or a public benefactor, an ally of the laws (the Sycophant's self-description at *Wealth* 911–915), was a man who felt confident in his ability to perform well in his time before the jury. His speech would not, we may assume, be rife with examples of *evitanda*.

Jury size and time allotments in the *dikastêria* varied according to the seriousness of the case. We do know that the *dikastêria* were convened at least 150 days each year. Mogens Hansen estimates that the juries were at work between 175 and 225 days, and that the number of dicasts empanelled

---

[24] Antiphon 2.2.12 is at least a likely reference to the practice of malicious litigation.

on an average day was 1,500–2,000, the exact number depending in part on that day's mix of private and public cases and the jury size required for each of them.[25] It is reasonable to assume that, other things being equal, the greater the proportion of small cases, the greater the number of *idiôtai* who appeared in court to speak for themselves without professional assistance. The complete text of Aristotle's *Constitution of the Athenians* might have held some precise information from which one might derive a more securely based estimate of the relevant numbers. The deplorable uncertainties in the text as it has survived deprive us of clean evidence, but I think we can at least make an informed guess.

The passages of the *Constitution of the Athenians* relevant to jury size and time allotments come at 53.3 and 67–68. From the first, where the text is complete, we learn that jury panels of 201 heard *dikai* involving sums up to 1,000 drachmas, panels of 401 *dikai* involving higher amounts. The opening of §68 offers the most potential help in reckoning proportions of the various sizes of jury. A hole in the papyrus is followed by a legible stretch: α τῶν δικαστηρίων ἐστὶ φ. "Five hundred" indicates that the author is speaking now of *graphai*. Wilcken had proposed filling the hole with τὰ δὲ πολλ, which would then yield the meaning "the majority of the courts are of 500 [jurors]" Kenyon accepted this reading in the OCT of 1920, but it is now universally agreed that more letters are needed to fill the space, and more recent editors agree on τὰ δὲ δημόσια, which would make the transition to public suits explicit but eliminate a remark on the typical size. Still, the text at least shows that private and public cases on the smaller side were important enough for the author of the *Constitution of the Athenians* to mention; moreover, the impressive workload of courts in session at least 150 times in a year to hear cases, none of which occupied more than a single day, makes it unlikely that the juries were empanelled for a docket of nearly nothing but very large cases.

Adjudication of *dikai* was sometimes suspended when public funds were insufficient to pay the juries (Lysias 17.3;[26] Demosthenes 39.17 and 45.4); this suggests a caseload that overwhelmed the system, particularly when the city's financial resources were under the added pressure of warfare. Other things being equal, the greater the number of cases, particularly the private cases that *idiôtai* would pursue more often than *graphai*, the greater the probability that poorer men would be coming to court and needing to speak.

---

[25] Hansen 1979, 1999:187 (cf. 188: "The passion of the Athenians for litigating and sitting in judgement is truly astonishing").

[26] The speaker's expression, "because of the war," is regrettably imprecise: see MacDowell 1971.

We should include under the rubric "dicanic" such procedures as *euthunai* (reviews of a man's conduct in office) and *dokimasiai* (hearings to determine eligibility): like cases of theft, assault, neglect of parents, or homicide, they involved individual citizens whose actions or status were assessed by a group sitting in judgment and empowered to order penalties. I have already mentioned the controversy over the authenticity of Lysias 24, a speech in which a supposedly poor man defends his right to a small public charity. There the man undergoing the procedure (probably a *dokimasia*) and potentially required to speak would, by necessity, lack the means to pay for a speech. All male citizens were subject to a registration procedure at deme level, and very great numbers indeed (over 700 each year) to the *dokimasiai* and *euthunai*, which were required of those serving as magistrates or members of the *Boulê*. The vast majority of these procedures were probably over and done with very fast, perhaps in less than a minute each.[27] But unless we are so credulous as to believe in the idealized view of Athenian day-to-day comity presented by Thucydides' Pericles in the Funeral Oration (2.37.2), irritations from private life must have sometimes erupted in the form of challenges at *dokimasiai* and *euthunai*, challenges that did not inconvenience exclusively the men of leisure who could function as *rhêtores* and *stratêgoi*.[28] It is more probable that procedures that became contentious but involved poor *idiôtai* – men speaking for themselves as best they could – would leave no trace in the form of professional speech.[29]

Many unhappy Athenian families might have been alike in generating conflicts for which the legal system offered at least the possibility of resolution. For example, there was a legal remedy for failure to care for one's parents (*graphê goneôn kakôseôs*), an action made less arduous and hazardous by the absence of time limits for oral presentation and the immunity granted an unsuccessful action (determined by the one-fifth rule) from the usual stiff

---

[27] *Euthunai* that "made the newspaper," a very small portion of the more than 1,200 procedures conducted each year, are collected in Hansen 1989:10 with n32.

[28] Preserved speeches written for *dokimasiai* involving challenges to election to office are very rare. All are Lysianic – 16, 25, 26, 31, and fr. 9 (for Eryximachus) – and date from the early fourth century.

[29] My guess is that challenges at *dokimasiai* for office were not as rare as Hansen supposes, hence I cannot fully agree with his summary remark at 1999:220: "*Dokimasia* must have been virtually always a mere formality, and to our way of thinking it must have been deadly boring; that the Athenians went through it year after year for centuries shows that their attitude to this sort of routine must have been quite different from ours. They evidently enjoyed participation in their political institutions as a value in itself."

monetary penalty.[30] It is perhaps significant that we have no speeches written for this action, though there are several allusions to it,[31] which may suggest that *idiôtai* were especially well represented in this form of litigation. And if a man died without having designated an heir, his estate might become the subject of a *diadikasia*.[32] Lysias 17 is unusual in that it is the only surviving speech for a particular form of *diadikasia* (Todd 1993:121), but the reference to the rhetorical challenge the procedure brought with it must have applied to many. The speaker opens (17.1) with an acknowledgment (or pretense) that he has ambitions that exceed his speaking ability:

ἴσως τινὲς ὑμῶν, ὦ ἄνδρες δικασταί, διὰ τὸ βούλεσθαί με ἄξιον εἶναί τινος ἡγοῦνται καὶ εἰπεῖν ἂν μᾶλλον ἑτέρου δύνασθαι· ἐγὼ δὲ τοσούτου δέω περὶ τῶν μὴ προσηκόντων ἱκανὸς εἶναι λέγειν, ὥστε δέδοικα μὴ καὶ περὶ ὧν ἀναγκαῖόν μοί ἐστι, ἀδύνατος ὦ τὰ δέοντα εἰπεῖν. οἴομαι μὲν οὖν, ἐὰν πάντα διηγήσωμαι τὰ πεπραγμένα ἡμῖν πρὸς Ἐράτωνα καὶ τοὺς ἐκείνου παῖδας, ῥᾳδίως ἐξ αὐτῶν ὑμᾶς εὑρήσειν ἃ προσήκει σκέψασθαι περὶ ταύτης τῆς διαδικασίας.

Because of my desire to make a name for myself, gentlemen of the jury, some of you may think I could also speak better than other people. In fact I am so far from being competent to speak about things that do not concern me that I fear I may be incapable of saying what is necessary even about matters I must talk about. Nevertheless, if I give you a full account of our dealings with Eraton and his children, I think you will easily discover what attitude you should take towards this adjudication [*diadikasia*].

Whatever the truth about what this speaker might do working on his own, his very statement of incapacity has been written for him by a prominent *logographos*. But this fact does not make it any less likely that many Athenians were forced to speak without expensive assistance or else forgo their claims to an inheritance.[33]

---

[30] Aristotle *Constitution of the Athenians* 56.6 and Harpocration svv. κακώσεως and εἰδαγγελία.

[31] Including Isaeus 1.39, 8.32; Demosthenes 35.47–48; Hyperides *In Defense of Euxenippos* 6.

[32] The range of this procedure is controversial: see Harrison 1968:1.214–217.

[33] An important aspect of inheritance, the adjudication of disputes over the marriage of an *epiklêros* (a woman "attached" to an estate, but disbarred from controlling it), presents a similar picture: a situation that is likely to have forced an *idiôtês* to speak without professional assistance.

I close this chapter with a caution. We must not forget that we do not know the degree to which litigants, regardless of their economic status, relied on themselves, the assistance available gratis from friends and relatives, the confidence they felt in their own persuasive powers, and whatever profit they could draw from written materials. Finally, we should not erect too high a wall between forensic speech occasions per se and the meetings that came before, and sometimes obviated, sessions of the *dikastêria*. According to the *Constitution of the Athenians* litigants were obliged to present all the "laws, challenges, and evidence" that they intended to present at court if the arbitration failed (53.3). Arbitration and pre-trial sessions were in themselves less demanding than court appearances, since they were not public events, viewed by a large jury and spectators (e.g. Demosthenes 47.12) and precisely timed. Since arbitration was a service required of all Athenian men as they left the military ranks (*Constitution of the Athenians* 53.4–6), and these men were not all adept readers, it cannot be the case that litigants simply put copies of documents down on a table and allowed the written words to speak for themselves; hence, they did require speaking about contentious happenings, and the outcome was unpredictable and potentially momentous.[34] My guess is that men saw even these preliminary meetings as requiring as much careful and persuasive speech as they could muster, whether on their own or with professional help.[35]

---

[34] If an appearance before one of the Forty over a matter of less than ten drachmas stands at one extreme, participation in a public action involving the city's most powerful men stands at the other: see Rubinstein 2000:192–193, who discusses the possibility of non-elite participation in the form of *sunêgoria*.

[35] The inherent theatricality or "staginess" of legal confrontation has received much attention since the 1980s, but I see a danger of circularity in assuming that the frequent use of legal motifs in tragedies and comedies (especially New Comedy) not explicitly centered on rhetoric and the institutions of justice can by itself supply evidence that real Athenians, the poor as well as the rich, had what Adele Scafuro calls a "forensic disposition" (Scafuro 1997:9–10, 25–27, and passim). I much regret the need to abstain from this material, particularly since it shows characters casting their speech in recognizably legal form in anticipation or in the immediate aftermath of a confrontation.

3

NATURAL AND ARTIFICIAL SPEECH FROM HOMER TO HYPERIDES: A BRIEF SKETCH

From Homer to the Mid-Fifth Century

THE CONTINUITY OF GREEK RHETORICAL TRADITION has become controversial, with much of the controversy centering around those Plato identifies as teachers of rhetoric in the *Phaedrus*.[1] Others take a broader view and see abundant material in the earliest texts, including Homer and the Homeric hymns. I have nothing to contribute here to the question of the definition of rhetoric, but will only present a few passages, most of them obligatory items in any survey of persuasive speech, that confirm the antiquity, at least in Greek "high culture," of several notions of public speech before the advent of the canonical Athenian texts: style as an index of a speaker's intrinsic worthiness, skilled and unskilled speech, natural and artificial speech, and the role of instruction and practice in the development of speech style.

The testimony of archaic Greece is unanimous: poetic skill is a divine gift, often bestowed on a man in an epiphany he can later make the very subject of a song, as in the proem of Hesiod's *Theogony*, or in anecdotes told about the poets, for instance the story of Archilochus' encounter with the "fat ladies."[2] Eloquent speech might be a gift presented at birth:

Καλλιόπη θ᾽· ἡ δὲ προφερεστάτη ἐστὶν ἁπασέων.
ἡ γὰρ καὶ βασιλεῦσιν ἅμ᾽ αἰδοίοισιν ὀπηδεῖ.
ὅντινα τιμήσουσι Διὸς κοῦραι μεγάλοιο
γεινόμενόν τε ἴδωσι διοτρεφέων βασιλήων,
τῷ μὲν ἐπὶ γλώσσῃ γλυκερὴν χείουσιν ἐέρσην,

---

[1] Cole 1991, a challenge to the orthodox opinion, sees "rhetoric" in the sense of discursive treatment of persuasive speech, rather than model texts, as starting only with Plato's *Phaedrus*.
[2] Preserved in the Mnesiepes Inscription (Archilochus T 4.27–30 Tarditi).

τοῦ δ' ἔπε' ἐκ στόματος ῥεῖ μείλιχα· οἱ δέ νυ λαοὶ
πάντες ἐς αὐτὸν ὁρῶσι διακρίνοντα θέμιστας
ἰθείῃσι δίκῃσιν·

Calliope, preeminent among all [the Muses], since she accompanies the respected kings. Whomever of the god-nourished kings the daughters of great Zeus honor and mark out at his birth, on his tongue they pour sweet dew, and from his lips words flow like honey. And the people look upon him as he administers the rules with straight judgments.

Hesiod *Theogony* 79–86

On this account, beauty of speech is a divine gift, selectively bestowed on certain well-born men.[3] The people appreciate such speech for its aesthetic qualities, which are in fact employed for just ends.

Hesiod does not here portray eloquence as granted even to all aristocrats. In Homer the few relevant passages suggest that even the best born might not speak well without instruction. That is at least one interpretation of Phoenix's words to Achilles at *Iliad* 9.442–443:

τοὔνεκά με προέηκε διδασκέμεναι τάδε πάντα,
μύθων τε ῥητῆρ' ἔμεναι πρηκτῆρά τε ἔργων.

For this reason [your father] sent me to teach you all things, to be both a speaker of words and a doer of deeds.

These words might, just possibly, refer exclusively to content, perhaps matters of strategy.

There is no ambiguity, however, in Antenor's description (*Iliad* 3.216–22) of how Menelaus and Odysseus spoke when they came to Troy, presumably to negotiate Helen's return. Antenor commends Menelaus' speech for excelling in what we might suppose were the usual criteria, clarity and persuasiveness:

ἀλλ' ὅτε δὴ πολύμητις ἀναΐξειεν Ὀδυσσεὺς
στάσκεν, ὑπαὶ δὲ ἴδεσκε κατὰ χθονὸς ὄμματα πήξας,
σκῆπτρον δ' οὔτ' ὀπίσω οὔτε προπρηνὲς ἐνώμα,
ἀλλ' ἀστεμφὲς ἔχεσκεν ἀΐδρεϊ φωτὶ ἐοικώς·

---

[3] Two readers tell me that they doubt that Hesiod means that the people admire the kings' eloquence, "rather than the beauty of their judgments." I cannot see how sweetness of divinely endowed speech can be treated as merely a metaphor for appreciation of content alone after the poet describes the effect of their gift as localized in the vocal mechanism.

φαίης κε ζάκοτόν τέ τιν' ἔμμεναι ἄφρονά τ' αὔτως.
ἀλλ' ὅτε δὴ ὄπα τε μεγάλην ἐκ στήθεος εἵη
καὶ ἔπεα νιφάδεσσιν ἐοικότα χειμερίῃσιν,
οὐκ ἂν ἔπειτ' Ὀδυσῆΐ γ' ἐρίσσειε βροτὸς ἄλλος·

But when wily Odysseus leaped up, he stood there, his eyes fixed on the ground, and looked up from under his eyebrows. He did not move the scepter back and forth, but held it immobile, like an ignorant man. You could say that he was surly and witless. But when his voice came, loud, from his chest, his words like snow, no other man could compete with Odysseus.

There was, then, a way one was expected to speak, or at least to wield the scepter, the physical object that, as it were, gave one the floor. Odysseus succeeds in part by playing off against an established mode to trick his audience into taking him for a dolt, or at least an amateur in the grip of embarrassment and fear.[4]

Odysseus glares at Thersites, the non-aristocrat par excellence, with the same up-from-below look (*Iliad* 2.245), and after a bit of sarcastic praise (λιγύς περ ἐὼν ἀγορητής, "though you are a clear-voiced speaker" [*Iliad* 2.246]), joins the poet (*Iliad* 2.213–214) in excoriating him for his disorderly speech. In general, a speech can be disordered on the level of content or style. As Thersites' speech repeats lines already spoken by Achilles (*Iliad* 1.232 = 2.242; 1.356–357 = 2.240), one might exonerate at least that part of the content that speaks of the dishonor Agamemnon has done Achilles. Thersites' speaking voice is characterized as loud, presumably too loud, and shrill (*Iliad* 2.223–224), two qualities skilled speakers of the classical period worked to avoid. (Of course, Thersites has also offended speech protocol simply by addressing the army without having been given the scepter, a point made explicit only when Odysseus beats him with it [*Iliad* 2.245].)[5]

Solon, the first Athenian whose own words are preserved (Antiphon will be the next – more than a hundred years later), had a choice between poetry and prose. He chose the more artificial form:

αὐτὸς κῆρυξ ἦλθον ἀφ' ἱμερτῆς Σαλαμῖνος,
κόσμον ἐπ<έω>ν †ὠιδὴν ἀντ' ἀγορῆς θέμενος.

---

[4] Commentators do not agree on precisely what the comparison to snow is meant to convey. In any case, the delivery was something very unusual.

[5] Regrettably, there is no mention of speech style in the description of a legal procedure on the shield of Achilles (*Iliad* 18.497–508).

I have come as a herald from fair Salamis, having composed a song,
ornament of words, in place of a speech.

Solon fr. 1 West

I think it just possible that the word κόσμον was meant not only as a way of
denoting verse, in this instance elegiac couplets, but for its suggestion of an
orderliness in expression that comported with the orderliness of the speaker
and his political agenda.

In another elegiac poem, Solon berates the Athenians for quite literally misapprehending the wiliness of "a man," presumably Pisistratus. When
assembled in a mass and listening to his words, they abandon their usual individual good judgment by ignoring the testimony of their own eyes:

ὑμέων δ' εἷς μὲν ἕκαστος ἀλώπεκος ἴχνεσι βαίνει,
σύμπασιν δ' ὑμῖν χαῦνος ἔνεστι νόος·
ἐς γὰρ γλῶσσαν ὁρᾶτε καὶ εἰς ἔπη αἱμύλου ἀνδρός,
εἰς ἔργον δ' οὐδὲν γιγνόμενον βλέπετε.

Each one of you follows in the footsteps of the fox; everyone's mind
is empty. You gaze at the tongue and words of a crafty man, but do
not look at any of his deeds.

Solon fr. 11.5–8 West

This fragment has a certain historical value as an early reference to syn-
aesthesia, here the sense of sight yielding its place to the sense of hearing
(cf. Cleon's complaint at Thucydides 3.38.4). A curious irony is that Pisistratus
is likely to have make a pitiable display of his wounds, falsely attributed to his
enemies – a visual datum (see Plutarch *Life of Solon* 30). If so, Pisistratus would
have exploited the Athenians' sense of sight, and the *ergon* to which Solon
would direct their gaze would have to be something else. It also speaks, though
not with any specificity, of an effect attributed to a large audience.

As we round the corner into the fifth century, we encounter several
prosecutions of prominent politicians that might have called for the *genos
dikanikon*,[6] but fate has robbed us of the sort of evidence useful for this study.
Miltiades was the defendant in the first two actions, but we know nothing
of the speeches made before, respectively, the *dikastêrion* and the Ecclesia
that heard the cases. Indeed, Herodotus (6.136) reports that at the Ecclesia
Miltiades, too sick to speak, left the defense to be spoken by his friends as he

---

[6] The historical facts are conveniently tabulated at Hansen 1975:69–70.

lay on a stretcher. Even if he labored to wring the maximum advantage from the piteous sight, it was insufficient to win his acquittal.

Plutarch relates a charming (or perhaps horrifying) anecdote about the boy Themistocles playing a sort of forensic solitaire:

> However humble his birth, it is generally agreed that as a boy he was impetuous, naturally clever, and strongly drawn to a life of action and public service. Whenever he was on holiday or had time to spare from his lessons, he did not play or idle like the other boys, but was always to be found composing or rehearsing speeches by himself. These took the form of a prosecution or defense of the other boys, so that his teacher remarked to him more than once: "At least there will be nothing petty about you, my boy. You are going to be a great man one way or the other, either for good or evil."

> *Life of Themistocles* 2.1–2 (trans. Scott-Kilvert,
> with slight adaptations)

Not a story to be taken seriously, except perhaps as showing what later generations would consider a plausible event in the life of this particular boy. Only a little less easy to dismiss is Plutarch's account toward the end of the same chapter of instruction in oratory Themistocles took from Mnesiphilus:

> This man was neither an orator nor one of the so-called natural philosophers, but had made a special study of what at that time went by the name of "wisdom" [*sophia*]. This was really a combination of political acumen and practical intelligence, which had been formulated and handed down in unbroken succession from Solon, as though it were a set of philosophical principles. His successors combined it with various forensic techniques and transferred its application from public affairs to the use of language and were termed Sophists.

> *Life of Themistocles* 2.6–7 (trans. Scott-Kilvert)

Thucydides, whose information on Themistocles' youth may not have been vastly better than Plutarch's, despite being some five hundred years closer in time, attributes Themistocles' expository success, presumably in symbouleutic oratory, to inborn talent, not instruction:

> ἦν γὰρ ὁ Θεμιστοκλῆς βεβαιότατα δὴ φύσεως ἰσχὺν δηλώσας καὶ
> διαφερόντως τι ἐς αὐτὸ μᾶλλον ἑτέρου ἄξιος θαυμάσαι· οἰκείᾳ γὰρ

ξυνέσει καὶ οὔτε προμαθὼν ἐς αὐτὴν οὐδὲν οὔτ' ἐπιμαθών, τῶν
τε παραχρῆμα δι' ἐλαχίστης βουλῆς κράτιστος γνώμων καὶ τῶν
μελλόντων ἐπὶ πλεῖστον τοῦ γενησομένου ἄριστος εἰκαστής· καὶ
ἃ μὲν μετὰ χεῖρας ἔχοι, καὶ ἐξηγήσασθαι οἷός τε, ὧν δ' ἄπειρος εἴη,
κρῖναι ἱκανῶς οὐκ ἀπήλλακτο·

Themistocles was a man in whom most truly was manifested the
strength of natural judgment, wherein he had something worthy of
admiration different from other men. For by his natural prudence,
without the help of instruction before or after, he was both of extem-
porary matters upon short deliberation the best discerner, and also
of what for the most part would be their issue the best conjecturer.

Thucydides 1.138.3 (trans. Hobbes)

This remark is likely to be an implicit rejoinder to those who preferred to
portray Themistocles as reliant on others.

Some decades later pity was again at work, if we can believe Plutarch's
account of Pericles weeping and begging the jurors to win the acquittal of
Aspasia (*Life of Pericles* 32.5).[7] Plutarch himself gives us reason for skepticism
about the anecdotes regarding Aspasia (24.12 and 32.6; see Henry 1995:16,
24–25), but even if the story is credible, Pericles himself was not a litigant, and
this fact clouds the issue of a speaker's self-presentation. Plutarch presumably
intended the story to illustrate both Pericles' devotion to his mistress and his
skill at getting his way with democratic audiences. (On the general matter of
appeals to pity, see chapter 6.)

"Tragic" Oratory from Antiphon to Hyperides

It is clear beyond question that no verbal art affected ordinary Athenians,
the men who manned the democratic juries, as intensely as the tragedies
performed at the city's dramatic festivals throughout the period of the
canonical Attic orators. Though it is often said that tragedy died with
Sophocles and Euripides in the last decade of the century, new tragedies and
revivals of earlier plays continued into the fourth century and beyond. Of
course, music and spectacle played a large part in the affective mechanisms
of tragedy, but the words alone played so strongly on the audience's emotions
that it would be strange if courtroom speakers did not sometimes look to

---

[7] Plutarch cites Aeschines Socraticus (fr. 25 Dittmar) as his source.

the vocabulary, phraseology, or delivery of tragic poetry as resource or inspiration.[8] Aeschines, himself a skilled actor, seems to have been particularly inclined to make such borrowings, but at the risk of exposing himself to his opponents' ridicule. In 346/5, Demosthenes quoted (or pretended to quote) Aeschines (19.189):

"ποῦ δ' ἅλες; ποῦ τράπεζα; ποῦ σπονδαί;" ταῦτα γὰρ τραγῳδεῖ περιιών . . .

"But what of the salt? What of the table? What of the libations?" That is his tragic lament . . .

The quoted words themselves, though metonymic in their function, are not proper to the tragic lexicon and they are not metrical, or even recognizably iambic in rhythm.[9] Presumably Demosthenes expressed his sarcasm by mimicking Aeschines' delivery in a style appropriate to the stage, but not an Athenian courtroom (see below n27).

I begin my discussion with some of the earliest preserved speeches, which conveniently exhibit the clearest examples of forensic rhetoric with (attempted) affinities with tragedy, other than quotations of tragedy explicitly identified as such or Demosthenes' partisan scoffing at Aeschines. Among professional orators, Lysias and his successors, I argue, were careful to avoid stepping out of their genre, as it were; I conclude with a short discussion of Hyperides, whom a prominent scholar has claimed made use of tragic language.

Antiphon

Sometime, perhaps around 425,[10] a man just old enough to take legal action on his own behalf stepped before the Areopagus and delivered a speech written for him by Antiphon in which he accuses his stepmother of poisoning his father. In the speech he wrote for his young client, Antiphon (1.1) has him

---

[8] Aristotle's *Rhetoric* surprises modern readers with its frequent quotation of tragic lines, particularly by the fourth-century rhetorician and poet Theodectes. This does not mean that Aristotle or those who may have had a part in producing the text of the *Rhetoric* expected speakers to compose, or even often quote, tragic lines: ῥυθμὸν δεῖ ἔχειν τὸν λόγον, μέτρον δὲ μή· ποίημα γὰρ ἔσται ("Speech should have rhythm, but not meter, for if it does it will become a poem," 1408b30–31).

[9] Aeschines 2.22 attributes "salt" and "table" to Demosthenes' own expostulations.

[10] Usher 1999:27 writes, "There has been little scholarly opposition to the tentatively expressed opinion of Blass . . . that the speech *Against the Stepmother* is the earliest," but cf. Dover 1950:49–53.

open with an emphatic statement of the duress under which he is addressing the court:

> νέος μὲν καὶ ἄπειρος δικῶν ἔγωγε ἔτι, δεινῶς δὲ καὶ ἀπόρως ἔχει
> μοι περὶ τοῦ πράγματος, ὦ ἄνδρες, τοῦτο μὲν εἰ ἐπισκήψαντος τοῦ
> πατρὸς ἐπεξελθεῖν τοῖς αὐτοῦ φονεῦσι μὴ ἐπέξειμι, τοῦτο δὲ εἰ
> ἐπεξιόντι ἀναγκαίως ἔχει οἷς ἥκιστα ἐχρῆν ἐν διαφορᾷ καταστῆναι,
> ἀδελφοῖς ὁμοπατρίοις καὶ μητρὶ ἀδελφῶν.

> I am still so young and inexperienced in legal matters, gentlemen,
> that I face a terrible dilemma in this case: either I fail in my duty to
> my father, who instructed me to prosecute his murderers, or, if I do
> prosecute, I am forced to quarrel with people who should least of all
> be my opponents – my own half-brothers and those brothers' mother.

Just before ending his speech (§§29–30), he refers again to the prosecution of his stepmother as undertaken in obedience to his father, but now adding two pathetic details: his father was dying when he gave his son the order to seek vengeance, and he himself was still a boy (παῖς) at the time. My contention is that Antiphon witnessed, and probably experienced himself, the strong emotional effects tragedians worked on their audience; because his client was a novice, and the young man's case was weak, he elected to raise the rhetorical temperature. The narrative is especially rich in such features, among them:

— the speaker's referring to his stepmother as "Clytemnestra" (§17)

— a stretch of iambic rhythm at §19: ἡ δὲ παλλακὴ τοῦ Φιλόνεω
τὴν σπονδὴν

ἅμ᾽ ἐγχέουσ᾽ ἐκείνοις εὐχομένοις ἃ οὐκ ἔμελλε τελεῖσθαι,

— similarly at §20: ἐκπίνουσιν ὑστάτηνν πόσιν (see Barigazzi 1955)

— the use of words in a sense they bear almost exclusively in poetry:
ἐπίχειρα for 'punishment' and ἤδη for 'forthwith' (see Gagarin 1997)

— the use of a historical present at §20 (see Barigazzi 1955), in the manner of a Euripidean messenger speech[11]

---

[11] Gagarin cites de Jong 1991:38–45.

— the description of the disguised poison as a human killer (φονεύς) at §20.

Against the Stepmother is not unique among the speeches attributed to Antiphon for the occurrence of poeticisms: see especially Cucuel 1886:22–23.[12] And there is a degree of emotionalism in all of them, even in the *Tetralogies*, which have no direct connection to actual persons and events. Nevertheless, the concentration of affective features found in *Against the Stepmother* cannot be paralleled in any other logographic text.[13] Perhaps if we had his complete oeuvre we would be less startled by blanket descriptions of Antiphon's style as eschewing emotion, e.g. Caecilius as quoted in [Plutarch] *Lives of the Ten Orators* 832 E5, assuming this text is correct in supplying the negating word οὐ, which is underlined in the Greek and in the translation:[14]

Καικίλιος δ' ἐν τῷ περὶ αὐτοῦ συντάγματι Θουκυδίδου τοῦ συγ-
γραφέως καθηγητὴν τεκμαίρεται γεγονέναι ἐξ ὧν ἐπαινεῖται παρ'
αὐτῷ ὁ Ἀντιφῶν. ἔστι δ' ἐν τοῖς λόγοις ἀκριβὴς καὶ πιθανὸς καὶ
δεινὸς περὶ τὴν εὕρεσιν καὶ ἐν τοῖς ἀπόροις τεχνικὸς καὶ ἐπιχειρῶν
ἐξ ἀδήλου καὶ ἐπὶ τοὺς νόμους καὶ <u>οὐ</u> τὰ πάθη τρέπων τοὺς λόγους
τοῦ εὐπρεποῦς μάλιστα στοχαζόμενος.

In his treatise on Antiphon, Caecilius concludes from Thucydides' praise of Antiphon that he was Thucydides' teacher. Antiphon is

---

[12] His list is based strictly on distribution by genre, which is not in my view a sufficient criterion: see Bers 1984:10 on φροῦδος and the extended vocative I quote there, *Tetralogy* 2.3.3: ὦ ἄνδρες ἀνοσίων ἔργων τιμωροί, ὁσίων δὲ διαγνώμονες (incorrectly attributed to 6.1; cf. *Tetralogy* 1.2.13), that I believe recalls the extended vocative phrases familiar in tragedy, and so is likely to be felt as meant to recall tragedy's stylistic level.

[13] The press's reader asks whether Lysias 32 *Against Diogeiton* might not be similar. The abbreviated text preserved by Dionysius of Halicarnassus certainly has drama, in the nontechnical sense of the word, particularly in the long *oratio recta* quotation of the speaker's mother at §§15–17 (Bers 1997:185–186; Usher 1999:80–82). But even in this speech, Lysias does not use the linguistic devices specific to tragedy. In his commentary (1989:208) Carey speaks of Lysias' "restrained use of overt appeal to emotion," which seems an accurate formulation.

[14] Gernet supplied οὐ, which is printed by Mau in the Teubner (1971). Aside from any consideration of how the author of this spurious work viewed Antiphon, the internal logic of the sentence seems to me to require the negative; if the point was really that the appeal to emotion did not compromise the dignity of the writing, I would expect some explicit concessive marker, e.g. καίπερ. Cuvigny in his Budé edition of Plutarch *Moralia* (Paris, 1981) removes Gernet's suppletion and rather mistranslates τοῦ εὐπρεποῦς as "impression de noblesse." Similar views of Antiphon's style as natural, direct, and orderly appear in two fragments of uncertain authorship in Photius: see Smith 1994.

precise [*akribês*] in speech, persuasive, and clever in invention,[15] skillful in difficult circumstances, stealthily going on the offensive, and directing his words [or arguments] to the laws, *not* the emotions, aiming above all at the seemly [*to euprepês*].

But the crucial difference between what Caecilius saw in the generality of Antiphon's style and what we see in Antiphon 1 lies in the immediate context, which provides a clear rationale for an affective usage, and thereby a link affording a very useful control for moderns, who must work by conjecture from scanty evidence. Contrast, for example, ὀπτήρ ('witness') at 5.27.3. The word is, as commentators say, of almost exclusively poetic provenance; but Antiphon's narrative at that point is objective and logical, hence not an appropriate location for an attempt at poignancy. We may conclude that the word was not chosen for its pathos – in the normal sense of the English word.

Similarly, ἄθλιος: as a glance at the LSJ entry for the word shows, it can apply to the cause of misery or, more frequently, a person suffering misery,[16] and its denotation therefore makes it a candidate for use in the complaints de rigueur in forensic oratory. Forms of the adjective and the adverb ἀθλίως are quite common in fifth- and fourth-century texts of various genres, but appear rarely in the *genos dikanikon* and other branches of oratory. The word is by its very meaning affective, but the distribution does not signal a specifically tragic or even more generally poetic word. Though there are many occurrences in tragedy (Euripides has over one hundred), its use in Aristophanes is not paratragic.[17] The word appears six times in Antiphon (once in a speech for a real case, five times in the *Tetralogies*), but though the passages are emotionally charged, ἄθλιος by itself does not appear unmistakably poetic. ἄθλιος, then, is not in the same category as, say, usages in Antiphon whose proper provenance is unquestionably poetic, e.g. ὁρῶσι τοῦ ἡλίου τὸ φῶς (1.68) or πρόρριζον (1.146).

The outcome of Antiphon's *Against the Stepmother*, like that of virtually all cases known from the surviving speeches, is unknown. I believe that the prosecution failed, not only because the case looked flimsy, but also because the emotionalism Antiphon instilled in the speech, far from compensating for the speaker's lack of evidence and inexperience, damaged the case further. This speech might be a statistical outlier in its concentration of affective

---

[15] For the technical meaning of the term see Kennedy 1994:4–5.

[16] A subsidiary meaning is 'foolish': see MacDowell ad Demosthenes 21.66.

[17] None of the nineteen occurrences of ἀθλ- in Aristophanes is cited by Rau 1967 as signaling paratragedy.

devices, comparable to few or none of the other professionally composed speeches heard or read in the first decades of logographic activity; but that it was Antiphon, as far as we know the preeminent *logographos* of his time, who had (if I am right) stumbled so badly would have made the impression all the stronger among those in the know, and above all among the other *logographoi*. I conjecture, therefore, that the affective style provoked distaste, possibly mixed with derision. Whether an outlier or not, the far more restrained style[18] exhibited by the other preserved speeches of the late fifth and early fourth centuries seems to me strong evidence that, other things being equal, an over-emotional style was likely to fail in Athenian courts.

Antiphon's preserved speeches are filled with devices or mannerisms that make his Greek distinctive. There is a streak of residual Ionic, especially in the *Tetralogies* (see Meillet 1975:237–241); he makes considerable use of doublets augmented by *homoioteleuton*; and with Thucydides, but no other prose writer, he shares a penchant for abstract expression, most notably in the use of abstract *nomina actionis* as the grammatical subject of a verb (see e.g. Denniston 1952:28–34; Gagarin 1997:24–32). All these features put his language at a considerable distance from routine Attic speech, without marking it as specifically emotional. The affective quality of Antiphon 1 derives almost entirely from verbal devices borrowed from tragic poetry. Obviously the speaker might have tried to amplify the poeticisms by a theatrical delivery, though we cannot often make that claim from the bare text: see the excursus on putative tragic features in forensic speeches later in this chapter. But the tragic theater was by no means the only place or occasion where an Athenian could hear men speaking emotionally. In the many courts of classical Athens one could, I will argue, often see men to varying degrees inflamed or stymied, even to the point of falling silent, when their turn came to speak. These were, for the most part, men who could not afford the full set of rhetorical armor provided by professional *logographoi*, and so had to rely on their own, often inadequate, resources. Of course, for all the advantages they gave, a good speech and professional training guaranteed nothing, as Antiphon's own fate shows (Thucydides 8.68.2).

---

[18] Often cited is Dionysius of Halicarnassus' characterization of Antiphon's style as "austere" (*On Literary Composition* 22.1), a term I do not find useful. In his influential book on the orators, Jebb (1876:33–34) sees both "tragic" and "austere" in Antiphon's style: "It is tragic, yet it is not dramatic. . . . The vinegar and the oil refuse to mingle."

Andocides

Andocides was not a *logographos* in the usual sense, since he is not known to have written any speeches for other men to deliver,[19] and his membership in the Canon has been regarded as unmerited, almost scandalous.[20] He too inserted some poetic words and phrases into his oratory. A few look like borrowings from tragedy appropriate to their immediate context,[21] but two are probably sarcastic ways of referring to his enemies' overblown accounts.[22] At 3.34, a symbouleutic speech, Andocides has an anastrophe of preposition, a turn that Aristotle mentions as a tragic usage, and not part of routine language.[23] Blass (1887–98:1.301) points to a single metaphorical usage at 2.2,[24] but the run of the sentence makes it clear that Andocides was at this point too being sarcastic, not poignant in the manner of the tragic stage.[25] And there are no other candidates for poetic, let alone tragic, borrowings in that speech. I see no reason to think that the outcome of Andocides' two forensic cases was much influenced by his stylistic choices.[26] How the juries saw his political activities and associations was probably decisive.[27]

Isaeus introduced (or reintroduced, if my reading of the style of Antiphon 1 and reaction to it are correct) a more affective style into professional forensic oratory sometime in the second decade of the fourth century. The freer use of oaths (see chapter 7) are an objective measure of this change, and perhaps we can put some credence in the ancient reports that speak of

[19] MacDowell (1962:19n3) remarks that "whereas And[ocides] was one of the last of the amateurs, Antiphon was one of the first of the professionals." Aeschines' professionalism, though acquired by nonconventional means (see Fisher 2001:12–16), was beyond question. There is no positive evidence that he wrote speeches for others, but in exile near the end of his life he well might have supplemented his income as a teacher of rhetoric ([Plutarch] *Aeschines* 840e) by doing some logographic work.

[20] Blass 1887–98:1.299 calls his inclusion "a marvel."

[21] E.g. at 1.68: ὁρῶσι τοῦ ἡλίου τὸ φῶς (a phrase one meets again in oratory at Lycurgus fr. 12.17).

[22] 1.29, οἱ λόγοι τῶν κατηγόρων ταῦτα τὰ δεινὰ καὶ φρικώδη ἀνωθρίαζον, and 1.130, κληδών.

[23] εἰρήνης πέρι; cf. *Poetics* 1458b31.

[24] περικάονται of men waxing wroth.

[25] MacDowell's translation with the verb in question italicized: "I simply can't understand why they *flare up* so strangely if you're to get the advantage of some service of mine."

[26] As it happens, he failed in the first, Andocides 2 *On His Return*, delivered sometime between 410 and 407, but succeeded in the second, *On the Mysteries*, delivered in 400 or 399.

[27] Histrionic delivery can, obviously, make any word, even "salt" or "table," sound like an importation from the tragic stage. Whether or not Aeschines had in fact spoken in court in the manner he had used on the tragic stage, Demosthenes could at least claim he had done so, as at 18.13 (also of Aeschines): ἡλίκα νῦν ἐτραγῴδει; 19.189: "ποῦ δ᾽ ἅλες; ποῦ τράπεζα; ποῦ σπονδαί;" ταῦτα γὰρ τραγῳδεῖ περιιών . . . (MacDowell ad loc. explains the verb as "a sarcastic word for excessive lamentations, used here also because Ais[chines] had been a tragic actor").

his use of emotional appeals and his influence on Demosthenes (e.g. Dionysius of Halicarnassus *Isaeus* 3). But even the forensic speeches in the Demosthenic corpus, excepting those that are formally forensic, but in a deeper sense belong to the symbouleutic branch, do not exhibit the cruder expressions of emotion that I believe were common in amateur speech.

Excursus: Other Opinions on Tragedy and Forensic Oratory

Starting in the mid-1980s, many important discussions of the relation of tragedy to oratory have veered toward an inaccurate assessment of the role tragic poetry played in oratory. I offer here a highly condensed and schematized set of examples of this approach. My comments will center on forensic oratory, the subject of this monograph, but the overlaps between symbouleutic and dicanic cloud the issue when the speakers are prominent political figures battling their opponents in the *dikastêria*, as in all three surviving speeches written and delivered by Aeschines and the two corresponding speeches by Demosthenes, 18 *On the Crown* and 19 *On the Dishonest Embassy*.

One error, in my view, is claiming that evocation of tragedy – by which I mean precisely the plays so called[28] – is a motive for speakers' references to situations that might be compared to elements of tragic plot. In their remarks on Andocides 1 *On the Mysteries*, Ober and Strauss (1990:256–257) read the appeal (§§49–50) that Charmides makes to the speaker, his cousin, as "vaguely" recalling a number of tragic scenes depicting characters faced with terrible choices involving personal safety and the fates of friends and relatives. In "exciting times" – and the profanation of the Mysteries and the mutilation of the Hermae as Athens prepared to invade Sicily certainly made 415 exciting – such dilemmas, I insist, are rather part of real life. Ober and Strauss go on to say that Andocides "sees himself as someone who has suffered but learned through his vicissitudes," and that his words "call to mind the clichés of a tragic chorus." To my eye and ear – and I acknowledge that this matter cannot be decided by objective measures – the tragic passages they adduce lack the resemblance in content and form to justify this claim. A man's summary of his hard times, such as Andocides 1.144–145, cited by Ober and Strauss, is vastly different from a song performed by a group of twelve or fifteen dancers, metrically complex,

---

[28] Referring to Andocides 4.21–23 (its authenticity is controversial), where the speaker scolds the audience for treating real events as if they might be theatrical fictions, P. J. Wilson 1996:320 usefully distinguishes between "the tragic and . . . what might term the *tragedic* (that which relates to tragedy as a theatrical institution."

with vocabulary, phonology, and syntax that set it off from the spoken dialogue, itself strongly distinguished from routine language. Given that tragedies depict human beings reflecting on their ups and down (or in the case of the *Prometheus*, a divinity sympathetic to humans and one suffering human), we cannot on the evidence of choral reflection show more than that Andocides' experiences and tragic plots do not come from different universes.[29]

In the same speech, Andocides tells a lurid story of despicable abuse visited by Callias on his own family (§§124–128). He concludes the section by asking the jury what such a miscreant should be called – Oedipus? Aegisthus? Quite reasonably, Wilson cites this as an example of "the tragic . . . to some extent detached . . . from particular tragedies" (1996:317–318). The significant point, though, is that Andocides is trying to depict an enemy as a monster. This is the rhetoric of sophisticated name-calling, in a form far removed from the intricate craft of tragic poetry and, even more important, from the use of *mimêsis* to create an illusion that transports the audience to another world.[30]

The same point can be made even more emphatically about the occasional direct quotation of tragic passages, a practice well known from Aeschines (1.151–152), Demosthenes (19.247), and Lycurgus (*Against Leocrates* 100). Though there is of course no question that these trimeters are of tragic provenance, they are explicitly set off from the speaker's own language. Moreover, it is often the clerk, not the speaker, who actually recites some of these passages, and also passages from Homer and other poets. Observing that these orators are often queasy about introducing poetry, Ober and Strauss conjecture that they feared appearing to be giving "lessons in culture to the ignorant masses" (1990:252–254). Perhaps, but if the anecdotes about Athenian prisoners in Syracuse are to be believed, at least some ordinary soldiers and sailors knew passages of Euripides by heart[31] and would not have taken umbrage at hearing men of great stature (one of them an ex-actor) showing command of poetry, including poetry of the tragic stage.

In the course of arguing that there was "a certain displacement or readjustment of the sphere of theatre and politics," Wilson (1996:322–323) adduces Aeschines' complaint that under Ctesiphon's proposal Demosthenes is to be

---

[29] To their credit, the authors do some hedging. For instance, the "reference to cries and moans" that Andocides mentions at §48 "*perhaps* evokes a subliminal nod of recognition of similar behavior in dramatic choruses" (emphasis added).

[30] To put it another way, Andocides is not executing the deception (ἀπάτη) that Gorgias called an attribute of "just" tragedy (fr. 23 D-K).

[31] Satyrus *Life of Euripides* 39.29, Plutarch *Life of Nicias* 29. Taplin 1999:43 describes these accounts as "both positively plausible."

crowned in the Theater of Dionysus, just before the tragic performances, rather than in the Ecclesia's meeting place (Aeschines 3.153–156). In Wilson's elegant formulation, "The theatre has become the place of the tragic politics of Athens, and the disasters of Athenian international affairs of state are depicted in the shape of tragic scenarios." But I contend that these exploitations of the theatrical space by both Demosthenes and his circle and, with the valences reversed, by Aeschines, do not amount to a court speech that mimics the fundamental mechanics of tragic drama. Menander instructs the audience of his comedy to suppose that the "place is Phyle, in Attica" (*Dyscolus* 1–2); Shakespeare opens *Henry V* by asking the audience to let its "imaginary forces" transcend the narrow theatrical space and compress many years "into an hourglass." But an Attic tragedian never asks his audience to imagine that they are in the theater attending to the herald.[32] For an orator, even a former actor, to play off of tragedy is not for him to confuse the genres. In their practice, professionals evidently agreed with the complaint voiced by author of Andocides 4.23 and Isocrates at *Panegyricus* 4.168 that Athenians were more likely to pity characters in tragedy than actual human beings. Out of ignorance of this tendency, and desperate to persuade the jurors, the unaided amateur might have tried to mimic the theatrical mode – to his cost.[33]

At a more detailed level of lexicon, David Whitehead (2000:131n144) takes me to task in his commentary on Hyperides for not recognizing the orator's taste for "tragic flavoring":

> In his contribution to *Persuasion* [= Bers 1994] . . . V. Bers makes a measured but insistent protest against facile assumptions of rhetorical interplay between the lawcourts and the tragic stage. As in the volume as a whole, H[yperides] goes unmentioned, and Bers' thesis that, after the excesses of Antiphon 1, "forensic speech [was] purged of tragic flavouring" flies in the face of H's apparent liking for precisely that taste (cf. generally Pohle 53–6). What the present passage shows is him having his cake – deploring the importation of melodrama (literally: tragedies) into litigation – as well as eating it.

I see the cake, but not Hyperides eating that cake. The allusion to tragedy, or more properly mockery of an opponent for injecting melodrama on an inappropriate occasion, is clear enough, indeed explicit, in Hyperides and

---

[32] Aeschines 3.153: γένεσθε δή μοι μικρὸν χρόνον τῇ διανοίᾳ μὴ ἐν τῷ δικαστηρίῳ, ἀλλ' ἐν τῷ θεάτρῳ, καὶ νομίσαθ' ὁρᾶν προϊόντα τὸν κήρυκα.

[33] See the discussion at Halliwell 2002:213–214.

other fourth-century orators,[34] but Whitehead has not made it clear how in this passage or elsewhere the orator is exhibiting his *own* taste for tragic flavor.

More generally, Pohle's 1928 dissertation on Hyperides' language, *Die Sprache des Redners Hypereides in ihren Beziehungen zur Koine,* by no means demonstrates such a backwards-looking taste, but rather, as the title indicates, the relation of the orator's language to the developing *koinê*:

> Zusammenfassend ist über Laute und Formen bei Hypereides zu bemerken: Verhältnismässig zahlreiche Abweichungen von der üblichen Literatursprache des IV. Jh, verraten den Übergang zur *Koine.*

> In summary, we can remark on phonology and morphology in Hyperides that the relatively frequent deviations from the common literary language of the fourth century betray the transition to *koinê.*

> Pohle 1928:31

At the level of syntax, Pohle (86) observes that the imprecise designation of subject or object reflects the usage of everyday language.

Whitehead's claims that Hyperides exploits "the language of tragedy" (to use the rubric in his general index) are, however, almost all lexical. The section of Pohle to which he directs the reader, a list of words in Hyperides first attested in tragedy, is but one part of a chapter (pp. 33–60) that collects "new and unattic words," including words (a) attested only in Hyperides and grammarians, (b) attested in Hyperides and later authors, and (c) already attested before Hyperides in the Attic orators, and also found in epic, lyric, comedy, Thucydides, and inscriptions. This bouquet of authors and genres does not, of course, preclude a penchant for tragic language, but at the very least it should remind us that our knowledge of Greek lexicon is imperfect and that many apparent phenomena of word choice may be mere accidents of transmission (cf. Dover 1973:12–13 and 1975:125–126). As I argued in *Greek Poetic Syntax in the Classical Age* (Bers 1984:6, 11), inspection of the context provides a valuable control. If the general drift of the passage gives no motive for the presence of affect or elevation, as in, say, a narration or statement of fact in which we can see no reason for the speaker to stir the emotions or motive for him to indulge in stylistic parody, there is little chance that a lexical or syntactic usage is a poeticism. The role of affect is what I was particularly calling attention to in

---

[34] Examples at Whitehead 2000:130–131 and Wilson 1996.

the *Persuasion* essay.[35] To this principle we can add a further criterion: a court speaker's putative injection of a word drawn from tragic language and likely to be recognized by the jury as such is more probable if the word has a strong association with tragic diction, e.g. χθών for "earth" or, to take an example from Antiphon 1.21, ἡ εἱμαρμένη for "fate, i.e. death."

Let us examine first the words Whitehead has identified as an instance of tragic language, and then turn to others in Pohle's list of words in Hyperides that are first attested in tragedy.

> 1. *Against Philippides* fr. 21.7 Jensen (Whitehead 2000:58–59): κορ-δακίζων καὶ γελ[ωτ]οποιῶν. The second verb is attested in Aeschylus fr. 180 Radt, and evidently on that ground alone Whitehead writes that it "seems to have dramatic origins." Perhaps, but as Whitehead notes, that fragment might be satyric. Moreover, "capering and joking" (Whitehead's translation) does not suggest the characteristic (which is not to say inevitable) tone of tragic drama.

> 2. *Defense of Lycophron* fr. 3 Jensen (Whitehead 2000:98): πολλοὺς λόγους ἀναλώσω, "expend lots of words." "This particular metaphor appears to be of tragedic origin (Soph. *Aj.* 1049, Eurip. *Med.* 325), but in a courtroom context what speakers 'expend' is inexorably quantified by the waterclock." I am skeptical of any association with tragedy, and the temperature of the words certainly does not suggest drama.

> 3. *Prosecution of Athenogenes* fr. 13 Jensen (Whitehead 2000:306): περίφοβον πεποίηκας, "making me fearful." The first attestation of the adjective, Whitehead points out, is in Aeschylus (*Suppliants* 736), and he might have added that the passage is lyric. The prefix is not, of course, a high-style feature (the adjectival component without the prefix would be φοβερός). A strong word, certainly, but the context in Hyperides does not suggest high style. The speaker reports himself as so frightened that he turned to something he implies he would never have done under normal circumstances – throwing himself into assiduous study of the law.

---

[35] Bers 1994:189: "There is an abundance of poetic words at charged moments"; "The intense affect which contributed to success in one civic occasion, the tragic performance, was found to be unsuccessful in litigation."

4. *Prosecution of Athenogenes* fr. 22 Jensen (Whitehead 2000:312): ἂν ἐγγυήσι τις ἐπὶ δικαίοις δάμαρτα. That the noun δάμαρ ('wife') is archaic and poetic is beyond doubt, but the motive is exactly (and merely) what Whitehead himself points out: "the quotation or citation of laws." Tragic flavor is not at issue.

5. *Prosecution of Athenogenes* fr. 12 Jensen (Whitehead 2000:329): πρὸς δὲ τούτων εἰς ὠνὴν ἐνεσείσθην "'I was plunged into the sale'. This verb is apparently another of H[yperides'] borrowings from the language of tragedy. . . ." Whitehead objects to translations like Carey's "I was bounced into the purchase" as lacking in gravity. There are indeed many tragic attestations of the verb ἐνσείω and, what may be significant, no other fourth-century prose attestations. Moreover, the verb occurs in a passage Pohle could not know, Menander *Dyscolus* 583–584, where Simiche exclaims, ἐνσέσεικα θ' ἀθλίαι καὶ τὴν δίκελλαν εἰς τὸ φρέαρ μετὰ τὸν κάδοι, *might* signal one of those moments of silly mock tragic diction found from time to time in New Comedy – "Woe! Woe! I have dropped the dibble deep down into the bowels of this cruel well," as it were: the word ἄθλιος is very familiar from tragedy (occurring about 116 times in Euripides), and though found often in Plato, it is not common in oratory. But the very idea of a litigant portraying his imprudent buying of a perfume shop in tragic language, especially when the language of his narration otherwise looks entirely free of affect, seems to me improbable in the extreme.

6. *Against Demosthenes* fr. 7 Jensen (Whitehead 2000:30): . . . ὥστ' αὐτὸς ὑπὸ τῆς τύχης ἀφαιρεθεὶς τὸν στέφανον, ἡμῶν ὃν ἔδωκεν οὐκ ἀφείλετο. Whitehead writes (452) of the "tragedic origins of the imagery" and cites a number of relevant passages from Sophocles and Euripides. The literal bestowing of a garland as a mark of gratitude for beneficence to the city, which could include not much more than the satisfactory performance of a liturgy, was a very familiar civic event (see Demosthenes 18.120: exaggeration of how often the ceremony took place in the theater, Demosthenes' claims notwithstanding [see Wankel 1976 and Yunis 2001 ad loc.]). It therefore seems an unnecessary stretch to speak of a poetic image with an origin in tragedy or any other poetic genre.

Whitehead writes as if Hyperides employed diction otherwise consistent with the earlier, canonical Attic orators, but deviated from time to time take over words from tragedy, complete with that genre's elevated affect. I am not persuaded.

4

TERRORS OF THE COURTROOM

I n Demosthenes 22.25, a passage made famous by Osborne's 1985 article on the multiplicity of procedural routes available to prosecutors, we have one of the very few general references within a speech to the possibility that litigation, and specifically speaking in court, might intimidate some *idiôtai*:

καὶ μὴν κἀκεῖνό γε δεῖ μαθεῖν ὑμᾶς, ὅτι τοὺς νόμους ὁ τιθεὶς τούτους Σόλων καὶ τῶν ἄλλων τοὺς πολλούς, οὐδὲν ὅμοιος ὢν τούτῳ νομοθέτης, οὐχ ἑνὶ ἔδωκε τρόπῳ περὶ τῶν ἀδικημάτων ἑκάστων λαμβάνειν δίκην τοῖς βουλομένοις παρὰ τῶν ἀδικούντων, ἀλλὰ πολλαχῶς. ᾔδει γάρ, οἶμαι, τοῦθ᾽ ὅτι τοὺς ἐν τῇ πόλει γενέσθαι πάντας ὁμοίως ἢ δεινοὺς ἢ θρασεῖς ἢ μετρίους οὐκ ἂν εἴη. εἰ μὲν οὖν, ὡς τοῖς μετρίοις δίκην ἐξαρκέσει λαβεῖν, οὕτω τοὺς νόμους θήσει, μετ᾽ ἀδείας ἔσεσθαι πολλοὺς πονηροὺς ἡγεῖτο· εἰ δ᾽ ὡς τοῖς θρασέσιν καὶ δυνατοῖς λέγειν, τοὺς ἰδιώτας οὐ δυνήσεσθαι τὸν αὐτὸν τούτοις τρόπον λαμβάνειν δίκην. δεῖν δ᾽ ᾤετο μηδέν᾽ ἀποστερεῖσθαι τοῦ δίκης τυχεῖν, ὡς ἕκαστος δύναται. πῶς οὖν ἔσται τοῦτο; ἐὰν πολλὰς ὁδοὺς δῷ διὰ τῶν νόμων ἐπὶ τοὺς ἠδικηκότας οἷον τῆς κλοπῆς. ἔρρωσαι καὶ σαυτῷ πιστεύεις· ἄπαγε· ἐν χιλίαις δ᾽ ὁ κίνδυνος. ἀσθενέστερος εἶ· τοῖς ἄρχουσιν ἐφηγοῦ· τοῦτο ποιήσουσιν ἐκεῖνοι. φοβεῖ καὶ τοῦτο· γράφου. καταμέμφει σεαυτὸν καὶ πένης ὢν οὐκ ἂν ἔχοις χιλίας ἐκτεῖσαι· δικάζου κλοπῆς πρὸς διαιτητὴν καὶ οὐ κινδυνεύσεις.

Solon who made these laws, did not give those who wanted to prosecute just one way of exacting justice from the offenders for each offence, but many. For he knew, I think, that the inhabitants of the *polis* could not all be equally clever, or bold, or moderate, and that if he made the laws in such a way as to enable the moderate to exact justice then there would be many bad people about, but if he made it suitable for those who are bold and able to speak then private individuals [*idiôtai*] would not be able to exact justice in the same way. He thought that it was proper to deprive no one of obtaining justice, as each was capable. But how could this be managed? By giving many ways of legal action against offenders – for example thieves. You are strong and confident: use *apagôgê*: you risk a thousand-drachma fine. You are weaker: use *ephêgêsis* to the magistrates; they will then manage the procedure. You are afraid even of that: use a *graphê*. You have no confidence in yourself and are too poor to risk a 1000dr. fine: bring a *dikê* before the arbitrator and you will run no risk. . . .

(Trans. Osborne 1985:42)[1]

It is worth noting that although Demosthenes speaks of nonprofessionals and of poverty, he does not say what everyone probably knew, that a poor man most likely could not afford a logographer's fee. Roisman 2005:98 has a good statement on the ambivalences in Athenian opinions on the point:

To be sure, the orators did not criticize the poor for avoiding risky legal procedures, as they did the rich. Such criticism would probably have been considered unseemly and antagonized the jury. In addition, it is likely that the poor were not expected to take the same risks as the rich. Nonetheless, the poor, in contrast to strong, confident men of wealth, were seen as weak, fearful, and unable to defend their interests, their honor, or the public good in court.

There are also passages in which a speaker's complaints of unjust decisions touch on the class status of the litigants. Isocrates 18.9–10 is an often cited broad criticism of jury trials:

Some of his associates approached me and advised me to settle my differences with him, not to prefer defamation and risking a great deal of money [the speaker was a member of the liturgic class: §§58–59], not even if I really had faith in my case. They said that many things

---

[1] Osborne makes several important observations (1985:43): "there is no reason why the gratuitous information about social implications should be forced or false," that "strength, confidence, wealth and the lack of them are relative," and that Demosthenes' statement adopts the potential prosecutors' point of view, though there are "consequences for the defendant as well." For some important qualifications, see Carey 1998, esp. 98–109.

come out contrary to expectation in the courts and that your
verdicts were more a matter of luck than justice. . . .

This is of course a tendentious statement as it is attributed to his opponent's
side and is meant to explain the speaker's initial retreat from a court case. Still,
it is a useful reminder that fear of court appearances was a relative thing.[2]

Another passage in Demosthenes (23.5) speaks of a widespread fear of
speaking on public matters:

> . . . πολλοῖς τοῦτο φοβουμένοις, λέγειν μὲν ἴσως οὐ δεινοῖς, βελτίοσι
> δ᾽ ἀνθρώποις τῶν δεινῶν, οὐδὲ σκοπεῖν ἐπέρχεται τῶν κοινῶν
> οὐδέν.

> Many fear this: perhaps they are not adroit [deinoi] at speaking,
> though they are better men than those who are, and it does not
> occur to them to look into any matter of common concern.

Strictly speaking, the issue here is not explicitly forensic speech, but a
reluctance to speak in the political realm. That might be heard as a reference
to speaking in the Assembly, but the immediate context is the graphê at hand
(Rubinstein 2000:192 with n18).

Too well known to need documentation here are the many passages in
which a speaker asks the jury's indulgence because he himself, a man inex-
perienced in public speaking, cannot match his opponent's sharp skills in
what Shakespeare's Cordelia calls the "glib and oily art."[3] I turn instead to
indications of the specific challenges facing the unskilled speaker in an
Athenian court.

"Good Attic"

Lysias' speeches are written in that form of Greek we expect from other
evidence, inscriptions and Old Comedy. But the use of pure Attic in court
speech was not a long-established tradition. Antiphon, who was executed not
more than seven years before the earliest preserved speeches by Lysias, still

---

[2] From fear of punishment or material loss, defendants would, quite naturally, be less able to "do
themselves justice." Speechwriters sometimes make the point explicit, whether for themselves
(Andocides 1.6) or their clients: see Whitehead ad Hyperides In Defense of Lycophron 8.

[3] Cordelia is, of course, speaking straight, but within the ranks of professional speakers at Athens
there was much use of rhetoric complaining of the rhetoric of the opposition: see Hesk 2000,
chap. 4, esp. 227–231.

shows Ionic forms, even in those speeches he wrote for actual cases.[4] As we will see, native Athenians might have reason to worry about some specifics of their language, but foreigners had a more acute problem.

In almost its first words, Plato's *Apology* has Socrates ask the jurors' indulgence if, as a first-time speaker in court,[5] he employs the mode in which he was brought up:

ἀτεχνῶς οὖν ξένως ἔχω τῆς ἐνθάδε λέξεως. ὥσπερ οὖν ἄν, εἰ τῷ ὄντι ξένος ἐτύγχανον ὤν, συνεγιγνώσκετε δήπου ἄν μοι εἰ ἐν ἐκείνῃ τῇ φωνῇ τε καὶ τῷ τρόπῳ ἔλεγον ἐν οἷσπερ ἐτεθράμμην, καὶ δὴ καὶ νῦν τοῦτο ὑμῶν δέομαι δίκαιον, ὥς γέ μοι δοκῶ, τὸν μὲν τρόπον τῆς λέξεως ἐᾶν. . . .

Quite simply, I am, as it were, a foreigner when it comes to the style of speaking here. So just as if I were an actual foreigner, you would show forbearance if I spoke in the *phônê* [φωνή] and way in which I was brought up, *this* is what I am asking of you: to tolerate my way of speaking. . . .

Apology 17d–18a

The word φωνή sometimes refers to a language other than Greek (φωνὴ βάρβαρος) or a dialect of Greek, as in the expression at Plato *Cratylus* 398d: κατὰ τὴν Ἀττικὴν τὴν παλαιὰν φωνήν. Dialect is most certainly the meaning here, and the whole point of the sentence is more general, that Socrates cannot speak as a *rhêtôr* would. With the comparison, however, Plato is sarcastically rebuking the Athenian public, which he despised on intellectual, aesthetic, and ethical grounds, for their *intolerance* of what they took to be a dialect less suitable for use in their courts than their own. Plato's script for Socrates is mischievous, but not unique in its oblique reference to Athenian juries' attention to speakers' language. One passage from real forensic speech is reasonably certain to attest to Athenians' linguistic chauvinism:[6]

---

[4] Meillet 1975:241 speaks of "the difficulty with which Athenians' prose became Attic."

[5] The claim of forensic inexperience is itself a *topos* a *logographos* could insert for his client. For an extreme example see Isaeus 1.1, where the speaker starts off by claiming he has never even *heard* a lawcourt speech.

[6] Colvin 1997:306–307 does not see evidence in Attic comedy that the Athenians, or Greeks in general, supposed "their own [regional] dialect to be more *correct* than others," whereas "[t]here seem to have been (social) varieties of Attic which were regarded as less correct than others." *Pace* Colvin, I imagine that in an Athenian courtroom a litigant could try to provoke hostility to an opponent by blurring the distinction between regional and social variations.

ὑμεῖς δ᾽ ἴσως αὐτὸν ὑπειλήφατε, ὅτι σολοικίζει τῇ φωνῇ, βάρβαρον καὶ εὐκαταφρόνητον εἶναι.

You have perhaps supposed that because he makes mistakes in speaking [or "speaks in the wrong dialect"][7] he is a contemptible barbarian.

Demosthenes 45.30

"Unpacked," this suggests that the litigant does not speak good Greek, good Attic Greek, or that he is inferior by virtue of not being truly Greek and is perhaps to be despised as a slave (cf. Demosthenes 57.18). There can be little doubt that the close proximity of the notions is meant to bring the different ideas into close association in the jurors' minds.

On one interpretation, the defendant's poor Greek is the specific point of the insult at the opening of Demosthenes' *For Phormio* (36.1):

τὴν μὲν ἀπειρίαν τοῦ λέγειν, καὶ ὡς ἀδυνάτως ἔχει Φορμίων, αὐτοὶ πάντες ὁρᾶτ᾽, ὦ ἄνδρες Ἀθηναῖοι·

Men of Athens, you all see for yourselves Phormio's inexperience in speaking, that he can't do it.

My translation is deliberately ambiguous; Sandys and Paley think this refers to Phormio's "indifferent pronunciation," but Blass 1887–98:3.1:463 thinks bodily weakness and illness are meant. In any case, Phormio's undoubted ability to run a bank makes it unlikely that Athenians had great trouble understanding him.

But there is also some anecdotal evidence that the Athenians could be fastidious in matters of morphology or pitch accent. If we can believe the scholiasts' account of Demosthenes' deliberate mispronunciation of the word he claimed applied to Aeschines, μισθωτός ("lackey working for hire"), as a proparoxytone, even those Athenian present who favored Aeschines, simply because they could not tolerate an accent wrongly placed, were tricked into

---

[7] A glance at compounds of σολοικ- in LSJ shows the ambiguity: these words can refer to non-Greek-speaking foreigners (as at Hipponax 27 West), to "barbarous language" (Anacreon 213 Page *Supplementum Lyricis Graecis*), to a faulty construction in Greek, or more generally to poor manners or behavior. I wonder whether one element implied in the complaint reported by Thucydides (1.77.1) that citizens of cities in the Athenian League were compelled to litigate in Athenian courts was linguistic, that as speakers of non-Attic dialects they were at a disadvantage.

shouting out a correction, making it appear that virtually everyone accepted Demosthenes' characterization of his opponent.[8] And if we can believe an incident reported in the Suda without any indication of names or date, Athenians refused a financial beneficence for no other reason than that it was offered to them with an improperly formed future tense:

τοὺς Ἀθηναίους φασὶν ἀθρόους εἰς ἐκκλησίαν συναθροισθέντας ἐπὶ τῶν διαδόχων, ἐπειδὴ εἰς ἀπορίαν καθεστήκεσαν χρημάτων, ἔπειτά τις αὐτοῖς τῶν πλουσίων ὑπισχνεῖτο ἀργύριον, οὕτω πως λέγων, ὅτι ἐγὼ ὑμῖν δανειῶ, θορυβεῖν καὶ οὐκ ἀνέχεσθαι λέγοντος διὰ τὸν βαρβαρισμὸν καὶ οὐδὲ λαβεῖν τὸ ἀργύριον ἐθέλειν·

It is said that the Athenians were brought together at a meeting of the Ecclesia at a time of great financial difficulty. Then a rich man promised them money, saying "I will lend it [*daneiô*; correct Attic would be *daneisô*] to you." The Athenians jeered and would not put up with him because of his barbarous language and refused to accept the money.[9]

Suda s.v. Θεριῶ

The Athenians themselves did not all speak alike. Some, for instance, used verbal forms we are accustomed to deem "subliterary" or, to be more precise (following Colvin 2000:289), a "substandard social variety." Yet Aristophanes and other comic poets never ridicule the language of poor, uneducated Athenians who spoke that sort of Greek, though politicians whom the poet has chosen to slander, for instance Cleophon or Hyperbolus, are not immune. This might seem surprising, but it can be explained as a tactful abstention from jokes aimed at a great many of the Athenians sitting in the audience (Colvin 2000:293). There is no direct evidence for "incorrect Attic" issuing from Attic lips in Athenian courts, but Teodorsson has suggested that changes in the pronunciation of vowels – changes that educated Athenians resisted, but were soon to become became pervasive – were to be heard already in the classical period. Sommerstein 1977:62 regards it as at least possible that "the more prestigious pronunciation will have been used on all public occasions,

---

[8] Demosthenes 18.52. See Bers 1985:6n21; Yunis ad loc.

[9] Bonner 1927:164 refers to the speaker as a "banker of foreign origin," an unreliable inference from the word *barbarismos*; moreover, we cannot be sure that "one of the rich men" has to be a banker.

e.g. in court and in the theatre."[10] He notes the far-from-pellucid Aristophanic fragment that speaks of three speech styles: one "in the middle," one "urbane and rather effeminate," the third "not a free man's and rather boorish."[11] Whatever the precise features of this putative prestige language, an uneducated Athenian might have identified himself as someone who had not "been to school" as soon as he began speaking; and in the absence of a powerful class-consciousness among jurors who spoke the same way and regarded his speech as a call to solidarity, the man who spoke with an iotacist pronunciation, or whose language deviated in other ways from that of well-trained speakers, had yet another thing to worry about.

Delivery

The importance of delivery (*hypokrisis*) is a well-known theme. Especially famous is the anecdotal report that Demosthenes learned from an orator who had defeated him in political debate that the three most important things in rhetoric are, first, delivery, second, delivery, and third, delivery ([Plutarch] *Demosthenes* 845a–b). Other anecdotes are more germane to courtroom speaking. In one, a man planning to bring an action for assault goes to Demosthenes to ask for his help as a co-speaker (*sunêgoros*) and gives him an account of his sufferings. Demosthenes is (or more likely pretends to be) downright incredulous: "None of this happened to you." The man shouts at him, "None of this happened to me, Demosthenes?!" Demosthenes answers, "*Now* I hear the voice of a victim" (Plutarch *Life of Demosthenes* 11). But practice might cause the opposite effect, according to an anecdote about a man rehearsing a speech written for him by Lysias. The client finds his first run-through of the script very encouraging, indeed amazing; the second

---

[10] Sommerstein is by no means sure this is the case: "[I]f this kind of diglossia existed, would we not expect to hear more about it in comedy, which extracts so much fun from the dialects of non-Athenians and the half-Greek, half-gibberish of barbarians?" Dover's notion of tactful abstention from insulting the typical customer of Attic comedy would answer that question in the negative (Dover 1981).

[11] Fr. 706 K-A: διάλεκτον ἔχοντα μέσην πόλεως | οὔτ' ἀστείαν ὑποθηλυτέραν <τ'> | οὔτ' ἀνελεύθ-ερον ὑπαγροικοτέραν <τ'>. But Sommerstein acknowledges that phonology might not be the issue. The notion of an "effeminate" speech style might be relevant to my general argument, but I dare not adduce in its support a fragment this obscure. Teodorsson never mentions court speech, but does present evidence for consciousness of variations in synchronic pronunciation and training in the "better" pronunciation as early as the fourth century (1974:263–280). For other theories see Cassio 1981:92 (the "soft Ionic" in cultivated urban speech) and Willi 2003:160–162 (women as the "linguistic avant-garde," but cf. Colvin 1997:286: "what seems clear is that there was no recognized distinct women's language in Greece").

and third readings seemed dull and ineffectual. When the client complains to Lysias, he laughs and asks him, "Really? Are you intending to deliver this speech to the jury more than once?" (Plutarch *On Garrulity* 504c.) That litigants of any degree of experience had reason to fear their delivery might somehow fall short seems a certainty, even though much of the evidence is of the Roman period.[12] (In a discussion of appeals to pity in chapter 6, I consider some passages in Aristotle's *Rhetoric* that are often taken – mistakenly, I believe – to suggest that a good forensic orator was a histrionic orator.)

Abusive Language

Those accustomed to the strict decorum imposed on speech in most British and American courts, even at the lowest levels of the judiciary system, will probably be astonished on first encountering the pungent insults contained in many Athenian court speeches.[13] Particularly well known, in large part because it occurs in the most famous speech of the genre, is Demosthenes' description of Aeschines' mother as a notorious whore (18.129). To a surprising degree, however, the apparent ferocity exhibited by the *genos dikanikon* is, like the appeal to pity, something of an optical illusion arising from several causes. To be sure, we meet many allegations and innuendoes that a modern judge would instantly declare irrelevant, which is what one might expect of a legal system that operated without professional jurists empowered and qualified (for the most part) to suppress such material.[14] That situation would, on its own, reduce the "shock value" of some of the more lurid insults by lowering the threshold of permissible speech. Still, Antiphon and Lysias were remarkably restrained. Antiphon had his client refer to his adversary in *Against the Stepmother* as a "Clytemnestra" (1.17), evidently hoping to stir up in the jury the sort of visceral reaction they experienced in the theater (see my discussion of this speech in chapter 3), but his description of his father's death (1.20), an opportunity for lurid details and apposite vituperation of

---

[12] Lavency (1964) introduces the second anecdote on the first page of his book to illustrate the lateness of the evidence.

[13] There are compilations of abusive language in the orators (J. Schmid 1894/95, Opelt 1993). The latter has dragged a net so fine that it catches some very dubious fish, e.g. Andocides 1.47, ἀνέψιος. Carey 1999 is an excellent treatment, and its influence on this section will be obvious. Also frequent in court speeches, and irrelevant by our standards, are statements of praise and self-praise.

[14] Lanni 2005:113 argues that the homicide and maritime courts imposed "a narrower notion of relevance" than the popular courts. The latter of course constituted a much larger component of the Athenian system.

the defendant, is confined to stating the length of his illness. For a speaker to call the prosecution "most impious" (Antiphon 6.51) might look extreme to moderns, but the religious component of homicide procedure makes that sort of talk nearly inevitable.[15] Joannes Schmid's survey of Lysias (1894/95:8–12) concludes that he is not much more given to invective than Antiphon. It is not surprising that Lysias 12 *Against Eratosthenes*, written for himself to deliver, holds a large number of abusive words (only Lysias 14, *Against Alcibiades*, is richer in this respect).[16] Andocides goes much further than either. His condemnation of Epichares, one of his prosecutors, alleges prostitution and – a nice extra kick – a physical ugliness that presumably explains why his prices were low: "You were not just one man's boyfriend . . . you let anyone pay you a small sum, as the jury knows, and made a living in spite of your ugly looks." But it must be remembered that in the first generation of canonical orators Andocides is the odd man out, both because his speeches are less numerous and because he did not write for others (see the section on Andocides in chapter 3).

For frequent and ferociously expressed insults we must wait for Demosthenes and Aeschines. All of the surviving speeches by the latter and many of those by the former, even when part of the *genos dikanikon* in the strict sense, were an extension of their political struggle, and the hottest insults were directed against each other and their respective political associates, as in Aeschines' prosecution of Timarchus. Similarly, Apollodorus' attacks on Neaera in [Demosthenes] 59 are connected to his feud with Stephanus, and both men were heavily involved in Athenian politics. This is not to say that political vituperation was a joke, a game, or a sort of harmless shadowboxing in the "zero-sum" extended feud that some scholars have seen as the essence of the Athenian courts; my point is rather that men with no political ambitions, appearing in court involuntarily or in connection with some strictly private matter, could not adopt the same level of verbal aggression without a risk disproportionate to what was at stake. The jury might fear words of ill omen: "In a society where words have the power of omens, it is necessary to avoid utterances which may be interpreted as ill omened, as having the potential to precipitate an undesirable result" (Carey 1999:372). Some name-calling was proscribed by law and vulnerable to prosecution as *kakêgoria* (slander),

---

[15] In the same vein, J. Schmid 1894/95:6 remarks that the words μιαρία and ἀλιτήριος are pertinent to speeches on bloodshed.

[16] Andocides 1.122 contains what is, to my knowledge, the earliest attestation in oratory of the syntagma discussed at the end of this section. That passage could join the adjective βδελυρός in Opelt's list (1993:229).

but it was probably hard for an Athenian to predict how that law might come into play in any specific instance (see Todd 1993:258–262; Carey 1999:374–378). The professionals presented imputations of sexual wrongdoing very gingerly indeed (Carey 1999:379–386).[17]

We have a phenomenon that has long been explained as an imitation by the earliest preserved Attic oratory of the formality of Greek public speech as it appears in historians (see Appendix),[18] but we can go further. Professional speechwriters were playing a dangerous game, which they sometimes lost, when their accusations became strident *or* they missed an opportunity to capitalize on the jury's emotions. The historical Cleon (not, that is, the figure we know from Thucydides and Aristophanes) might have lost such a gamble in the Mytilene debate by working himself into a rant a few degrees too fervent.[19] It follows that amateurs more often lurched into the kind of abuse that would alienate the jury as a violation of good taste, as slanderous under the terms of the law, or perhaps even as inviting the invidious attention of a malignant supernatural power. Miscalculation would explain some of these failures, but I imagine that more often the fault lay in the amateur speaker's inability to control his anger or panic. The professionals watched the floundering *idiôtai* and learned to do better.[20]

Once a technical detail was introduced in a speech or group of speeches known to have succeeded in court, it might be imitated by other *logographoi*, or to a lesser extent, unaided *idiôtai*, with no further consideration of its rationale; that is, it might be perpetuated simply as a cachet. This process might explain some stylistic features that do not hold any very clear advantage in respect to manifesting self-control. A possible example is the syntagma εἰς τοῦτό/τόδέ/τοσοῦτον + a verb of motion + the genitive of an abstract noun usually denoting something reprehensible[21] + the supposed consequence. The construction occurs some 107 times in the Canon. Early examples occur

---

[17] Crudity appears to have reached its all-time height in professional speech at [Demosthenes] 59.108 – if the words "making her living from three holes" are genuine; see my translation (Bers 2003 ad loc. with n136).

[18] J. Schmid sees Antiphon's sparing use of invective as a sign of the high moral rectitude in public and private life admired in that era by the orator and the jurors of the Areopagus (1894/95:7). Schmid's naïveté (and class bias?) are remarkable.

[19] Hitler's public speech style, and even his hysterical-sounding delivery, were far from natural and unpremeditated; see www.dw-world.de/dw/article/0,2144,1360379,00.html.

[20] Not that the lesson was at all simple: "Although there are certain areas which require sensitive treatment, what can be said depends as much on the calculations and strategy of the speaker as on any fixed response from the audience" (Carey 1999:391).

[21] Euripides *Medea* 56–58, where the word in the genitive denotes something undesirable, but not contemptible, shows the construction from the point of view of the victim

at Antiphon *Tetralogy* 2.3.5.1 and *Tetralogy* 3.3.6.3: εἰς τοῦτο γὰρ τόλμης καὶ ἀναιδείας ἥκει, ὥστε ..., which we might translate more or less literally: "He has reached this level of audacity and shamelessness that. . . ." Its appearances in tragedy are limited to Euripides: Mastronarde (ad *Phoenician Women* 963) lists four Euripidean examples that take precisely this form, and four others with some semantic equivalent variant in place of the ὥστε component. Thucydidean speeches, by contrast, have only two instances to show. In Plato I count ten, and it is worth mentioning that three are from imitations of oratory (the *Apology* and the epideictic *Menexenus*) and three from the *Gorgias*, all in Socrates' mouth.[22] Xenophon has only one example. Paul Dessoulavy, savant of this construction, calls the phraseology "specifically rhetorical" (1881:3n1). This is probably correct, although it must be admitted that the earliest attested tragic example (Euripides *Hippolytus* 1332) dates from 428, perhaps contemporaneous with the example from Antiphon given above. Given the orators' general abstention from poeticizing turns, it does seem more likely that the tragedian is following the orators than vice versa. I agree with Collard 2005:378 (contra W. Schmid 1940:794n4) that the construction is not colloquial. To my knowledge, there is only one only comic example of the phrase with τοσοῦτο (Aristophanes *Clouds* 832–833), despite the genre's many opportunities to use it.

Timing

A speaker had to observe the time limits set for various private cases (Aristotle *Constitution of the Athenians* 67.2; see Wille 2001:1020–1021 for a collection of relevant passages). Within the speeches themselves we see a few acknowledgements of distress that the water level was dropping in the *klepsydra* and forcing the speaker to condense his plea or leave some points unspoken. There are complaints of time restrictions in real speeches (e.g. Demosthenes 45.47), but also some in a few that are probably (Andocides 4.10) or certainly (Isocrates 15.54) fictional, and even in epideictic oratory (Lysias 2.54). A number of speeches conclude with a formula expressing satisfaction, as it were, with the time allotted, e.g. Demosthenes 54.44:

> οὐκ οἶδ' ὅ τι δεῖ πλείω λέγειν· οἶμαι γὰρ ὑμᾶς οὐδὲν ἀγνοεῖν τῶν εἰρημένων.

---

[22] I would of course be more pleased to be able to report that they were attributed to the professional rhetorician rather than to Socrates.

I don't know what more I should tell you, since I think you understand everything that has been said.[23]

But even those words in the speech *Against Conon* are preceded with a claim often made, that only time prevents him from expatiating at great length on the merits of his case and the depravity of his opponent (54.44):

πόλλ' ἂν εἰπεῖν ἔχοιμ', ὦ ἄνδρες δικασταί, καὶ ὡς ἡμεῖς χρήσιμοι, καὶ αὐτοὶ καὶ ὁ πατήρ, ἕως ἔζη, καὶ τριηραρχοῦντες καὶ στρατευόμενοι καὶ τὸ προστατόμενον ποιοῦντες, καὶ ὡς οὐδὲν οὔθ' οὗτος οὔτε τῶν τούτου οὐδείς·

> There is much I could say, gentlemen of the jury, about how we have been useful to the city, ourselves and my father, as long as he was alive, serving as trierarchs and as soldiers and doing what was assigned, and useful as neither Conon nor his sons have been.

Isaeus has his client concede that the jury might be getting bored (7.43), and the Demosthenic *Funeral Oration* expresses similar a similar worry (60.6). Three times in the Demosthenic corpus (18.139, 19.57, 50.2) the speaker (twice it is Demosthenes himself) displays his confidence by offering to cede time to the other side with the words ἐν τῷ ἐμῷ ὕδατι εἰπάτω ("Let him speak in my time allotment").[24] But commonsense suggests that it was never easy to fill up all, or nearly all, the allotted time and still not get cut off. Not surprisingly, Alcidamas claims that the speaker trained in ex tempore technique – not, of course a man who can be counted as an *idiôtês* – will be best able to adjust the length of his speech to suit his audience "in real time" (*Concerning Written Speeches* 11.22–23). The careful planning and memorization of speeches look like countermeasures intended, in part, to cope with the challenge posed by time limits.[25] An amateur speaker, especially one with no accurate means to time his speech, no great ability to write out, read, and revise his speech – or perhaps no such ability whatever – and limited leisure to prepare, probably saw the *klepsydra* as a serious threat.

---

[23] Demosthenes 20, 36, and 38, and Isaeus 7 and 8 end with exactly the same words.

[24] I am sure Yunis 2001 ad 18.139 is right to say that "the offer is purely rhetorical." Cf. Dinarchus 1.114.

[25] I do not doubt that this is how the customers of *logographoi* prepared, even though the evidence is in the form of jokes and anecdotes, e.g. Aristophanes *Knights* 347–350 and Plutarch *On Garrulity* 504c.

Professional Delivery

To avoid some widely held misconceptions about the general character of rhetorical delivery and the scope of the Greek word *hypokrisis*, conventionally translated 'delivery', it will be best to move now to a discussion of the subject as it appears in the third book of Aristotle's *Rhetoric*.

Aristotle starts off by acknowledging (1403b15–16) that the way things are said has a large effect on the perceived quality of the speech, and that this matter requires attention not just in poetry, but in rhetoric as well (1403b24–25).[26] He continues:

> [*Hypokrisis*] is a matter of how the voice should be used in expressing each emotion, sometimes loud and sometimes soft and [sometimes] intermediate, and how the pitch accents should be entoned,[27] whether as acute, grave, or circumflex, and what rhythms should be expressed in each case; for [those who study delivery] consider three things, and these are volume, change of pitch, and rhythm. Those [performers who gives careful attention to these] are generally the ones who win poetic contests; and just as actors are more important than poets now in the poetic contests, so it is in political contests because of the sad state[28] of governments. An *Art* concerned with [the delivery of oratory] has not yet been composed, since even consideration of *lexis* [diction] was late in developing, and delivery seems a vulgar matter when rightly understood.

> *Rhetoric* 1403b26–1404a1 (trans. Kennedy 1991)

Aristotle soon repeats his complaint that the depravity of the audience is the reason for needing to attend to *hypokrisis* (1404a7) and then remarks, "Whenever delivery comes to be considered, it will function in the same way as acting,[29] and some have tried to say a little about it, for example Thrasymachus in his [account of] emotional appeals" (1404a12–15, trans. Kennedy 1991; see chapter 6 below).

---

[26] Here he must have all three branches of rhetoric (forensic, political, and epideictic) in mind, though at 1403b34 he remarks specifically about "political contests."

[27] I suppose this is not a misprint for 'intoned', but a word the translator has chosen to make it clear that Aristotle is suggesting the rising and falling pitch accents of Greek words, just the opposite of one occasional connotation of 'intone', to deliver in a monotone.

[28] Perhaps too mild a translation of *mokthêria*: see Chapter 1, note 7.

[29] *Hypokritikê*, the specific Greek term for stage acting.

For Aristotle, then, delivery (*hypokrisis*) is in large measure a matter of the speaking voice with no special connection to its use in drama. Others have, he reports, discussed the relation of rhetorical delivery to stage performance, but Aristotle refers to the matter only cursorily. I think it significant that in the *Rhetoric* he never uses *mimêsis* (imitation) or related words to describe a speaker striving to portray himself as a different person or to suggest that speakers should do so, even though many of his examples are drawn from tragedy.

Whatever the overlap in technique between orators and stage actors, Aristotle is far from recommending a histrionic style in court speeches. The *Rhetoric* cannot serve as evidence that those with the leisure and means to employ or work as *logographoi* routinely looked to the theater for instruction, even though by Aristotle's time the more restrained oratory of the first few decades of preserved speechmaking had in some measure given way to a decidedly more dramatic style, especially in the political oratory of the ex-actor Aeschines and Demosthenes.[30] In any period, *idiôtai* might have been drawn into conscious or unconscious imitation of tragic style, but for that I see no evidence.

Volume

Two stories about ancient speechmaking, famous enough to have reached many who know nothing else about classical rhetoric, are the accounts of Demosthenes' vocal training: shouting against the sea and rehearsing with pebbles on his mouth.[31] The anecdotes might be entirely fabricated or based on

---

[30] Hamlet's directorial instruction to the actor at III.ii.1–20 is weirdly Janus-like. A fifth-century *logographos* might have advised a client, "[D]o not saw the air too much with your hand, thus, but use all gently, for in the torrent, tempest, and, as I may say, whirlwind of your passion, you must acquire and beget a temperance that may give it smoothness." At the same time, the alternative to the traditional declamatory style can be said to anticipate the nineteenth-century revolution in acting. For a compact discussion of this famous passage, see Kermode 2000:113 and Kermode 2004:106–107.

[31] Ancient sources include Plutarch *Demosthenes* 6–7, 11; [Plutarch] *Lives of the Ten Orators* 844E–F, Quintilian *Institutio Oratoria* 10.30. Bien 1967 proposes that the story of the pebbles is a mangled version of his use of a stone as an obturator, a prosthesis to relieve a cleft palate, but as Lionel Pearson observed (conversation), in a period when taunting a man for physical deformity was not infra dig, Aeschines and his allies would not have hesitated to jeer at an opponent with a cleft palate.

misunderstandings, but the importance of delivery cannot be overestimated,[32] and the most elementary component of rhetorical delivery is volume. The most obvious concern would be speaking loudly enough to be understood in a large space before a boisterous audience, a challenge that fits the story of Demosthenes on the beach. There is, oddly enough, very little direct evidence for a speaker speaking too softly to be heard.[33] In a passage already cited in reference to speakers undone by audience reaction, Alcidamas uses the word ἰσχνόφωνος (weak of voice); best known, certainly, are Isocrates' own confessions of an insufficient voice. We can say more on the limiting case, as it were: a speaker who turns mute, an affliction I discuss in the next section. Simply speaking at length must have challenged the vocal instrument, as can perhaps be seen from a small bit of evidence for how a Greek might prepare his voice. At the moment in the *Thesmophoriazusae* when Mica is about to speak, the Coryphaeus hushes the group, explaining that she is clearing her throat "as the *rhêtores* do, for she'll be speaking at length" (381–382). Lysias opens *Against Eratosthenes* (12.1) by saying that starting his speech will not be difficult, but given the number and character of the respondent's crimes, bringing it to an end will be – something of a commonplace in forensic and other forms of rhetoric[34] – but at §61 he gives as a reason for the recitation of witness statements his need for a respite: ἐγώ . . . δέομαι ἀναπαύσασθαι ("I need to rest"). My guess is that although the admission is rare, and perhaps untrue in this particular instance, the need to rest the voice was familiar enough.

The common, if not nearly universal, fault appears to be just the contrary of speaking too softly – shouting. In the *Rhetoric* (1408a23–25), Aristotle says πολλοὶ καταπλήττουσι τοὺς ἀκροατὰς θορυβοῦντες ("many men blast their audience with their shouting"). One might say that these speakers turn the jurors' *thorubos* (heckling) back on them. Aristotle explains shouting as potentially enhancing a speaker's credibility: συνομοπαθεῖ ὁ ἀκούων ἀεὶ τῷ παθητικῶς λέγοντι, κἂν μηθὲν λέγῃ ("the hearer always shares the emotion with the man who speaks emotionally, even if he says nothing true"). The last phrase suggests manipulative cunning, as the speaker alleges of a puta-

---

[32] Pearson 1976:6. In that monograph and a number of articles Pearson advanced the theory that Demosthenes developed a vocal technique that made it possible to deliver very long phrases, very artfully adapted to his rhetorical aims; Dover 1997:178–179 is skeptical.

[33] Even the references to a weak voice (Isocrates *Panathenaicus* 10, *Epistula* 8.7; Alcidamas *Against the Sophists* 15) say nothing about the space and the number of auditors.

[34] E.g. Demosthenes 53.3. It can be found even if the speech is a fiction and the author horribly prolix, as at Isocrates *Antidosis* 15.54: ἅπαντας ἂν οὖν διὰ τέλους εἰπεῖν οὐκ ἂν δυναίμην· ὁ γὰρ χρόνος ὁ δεδομένος ἡμῖν ὀλίγος ἐστίν.

tively shouting opponent at Isaeus 6.59,[35] but I think it certain that men often shouted, or even screamed, out of genuine emotion or out of the simple fear of not being heard, and that they harmed their case thereby. If Plutarch can be trusted, Cicero was contemptuous of shouters:

... καὶ τούς γε τῷ μέγα βοᾶν χρωμένους ῥήτορας ἐπισκώπτων, ἔλεγε δι' ἀσθένειαν ἐπὶ τὴν κραυγὴν ὥσπερ χωλοὺς ἐφ' ἵππον πηδᾶν.

In mockery of speakers who shouted, he used to say that they screamed out of weakness, like cripples who jump on a horse [to disguise their inability to walk].

Plutarch *Life of Cicero* 5.6

The author of the *Rhetorica ad Herennium* likens a man's shouting to a woman's screaming (3.12.22; I know of no precise Greek parallel to this statement). Perhaps shouting tended to raise some speakers' pitch (see the next section of this chapter). Finally, some men might be carrying into court an ingrained habit of speaking too loudly. Nicobulus, who has brought a *paragraphê* (countercharge), claims that his opponent, Pantaenetus, is counting on a cluster of prejudices:

ἐπειδὰν τοίνυν τις αὐτὸν ἔρηται "καὶ τί δίκαιον ἕξεις λέγειν πρὸς Νικόβουλον;" μισοῦσι, φησίν, Ἀθηναῖοι τοὺς δανείζοντας· Νικόβουλος δ' ἐπίφθονός ἐστι, καὶ ταχέως βαδίζει, καὶ μέγα φθέγγεται, καὶ βακτηρίαν φορεῖ·

Now when someone asks him, "Actually, what claim will you be able to able to bring against Nicobulus," his answer is that the Athenians hate moneylenders, and Nicobulus is hateful, and walks fasts and talks loudly, and uses a walking stick.

Demosthenes 37.52

In context, the speaker's point is that Pantaenetus is elevating trivial mannerisms to the level of chargeable offenses, but there is evidence that those mannerisms were widely disliked and seen as symptomatic of a

---

[35] καὶ διαρρήδην μαρτυρήσας γνησίους τοὺς παῖδας εἶναι οἴεται ἐξαρκέσειν ὑμῖν παρεκβάσεις, ἐὰν δὲ τοῦτο μὲν μηδ' ἐγχειρήσῃ ἐπιδεικνύναι ἢ καὶ κατὰ μικρόν τι ἐπιμνησθῇ, ἡμῖν δὲ λοιδορήσηται μεγάλῃ τῇ φωνῇ καὶ λέγῃ ὡς εἰσὶν οἵδε μὲν πλούσιοι, αὐτὸς δὲ πένης, διὰ ταῦτα δόξειν τοὺς παῖδας εἶναι γνησίους.

detestable personality (cf. §55, and see Carey and Reid 1985 ad loc.). Perhaps Demosthenes was aware that his client was likely to exhibit the common court speaker's fault of fortissimo delivery; or perhaps Nicobulus was alluding to a general habit of shouting, which he was curbing in his court speech as a mark of respect for the occasion.

Literal aphasia is attested in a few places; more important, there is a probable connection to a phenomenon for which the evidence is abundant.[36] The opening of Demosthenes 36 *For Phormio*, discussed earlier in this chapter, might mean that Phormio tried to speak, but failed to make a sound. In the middle of his speech prosecuting Ctesiphon, Aeschines makes out that Demosthenes is speechless when offered the floor (3.166); just possibly he was flummoxed into silence, but Aeschines' ostensibly magnanimous offer at §165 to yield the *bêma* was probably not serious, hence Demosthenes had reason to refuse. If these bits of evidence from forensic speeches were our only evidence, skepticism would be in order, but plentiful corroboration comes from other sources, including comedy and tragedy.[37] A Euripidean fragment (fr. 88 Kannicht) describes the dread that overcomes a man on trial for homicide:[38]

ὁ φόβος, ὅταν τις αἵματος μέλλῃ πέριλέγειν καταστὰς εἰς ἀγῶν'
ἐναντίον,
τό τε στόμ' εἰς ἔκπληξιν ἀνθρώπων ἄγει
τὸν νοῦν τ' ἀπείργει μὴ λέγειν ἃ βούλεται.
τῷ μὲν γὰρ ἔνι κίνδυνος, ὃ δ' ἀθῷος μένει.
ὅμως δ' ἀγῶνα τόνδε δεῖ μ' ὑπεκδραμεῖν·
ψυχὴν γὰρ ἆθλα κειμένην ἐμὴν ὁρῶ.

When someone comes to speak at his trial for homicide, fear stuns his tongue and mind and keeps him from saying what he wants. For the one man [the defendant] there is danger, while the other [the prosecutor] is invulnerable. After all, I must elude this trial, since I see my life is the prize.

---

[36] I can find only one mention of a literal inability to speak in the capacious volume of Wille 2001 that treats the orators; it refers to fish, whose defect in this respect Aristotle explains as the absence of the requisite anatomy (823 with n75). *Praeteritio* and the like, which Wille does canvass, of course fall into a different category altogether.

[37] In what follows I draw heavily on Faraone's excellent 1989 article.

[38] I do not see why Faraone 1989:152 supposes that this discomfiture afflicted "[sc. only] those unaccustomed to public speaking." Given sufficient stress, the sangfroid that comes with experience will not always stay cool enough.

A scene from Aristophanes' *Wasps* (946–948) presents a dog afflicted by a canine form of aphasia: he cannot bark in his own defense. His misfortune reminds Bdelycleon of what befell Thucydides son of Melesias:

ἐκεῖνό μοι δοκεῖ πεπονθέναι,
ὅπερ ποτὲ φεύγων ἔπαθε καὶ Θουκυδίδης·
ἀπόπληκτος ἐξαίφνης ἐγένετο τὰς γνάθους.

I think he is undergoing what happened to Thucydides when he was on trial: he suddenly got paralysis of the jaws.

Citing a scholium on this passage together with the piteous tale of Thucydides at Aristophanes *Acharnians* 703–718, Faraone (1989:150–151) very plausibly suggests that the venerable politician, once fully capable of defending himself, was understood as the victim of two forces: a magical spell and the powerful rhetoric of younger men. He adduces several other instances of stymied court speech variously explained by ancient sources as brought on by panic (often augmented by courtroom *thorubos*) or a magic spell. Significantly, the mind and the voice – precisely the organs we expect a psychosomatic panic reaction to affect – are prominent among the body parts the judicial curse tablets target.[39] (For a tendentious claim, put in a sophist's mouth, that those addicted to philosophy will be at a loss if arrested and taken to trial on a capital charge, see Plato *Gorgias* 486a–b.)

In his two long speeches that arose from trials pitting him against Aeschines, Demosthenes ridicules his opponent's vocal qualities. His mockery, which centers on Aeschines' theatrical background, is two-pronged: Aeschines vaunts himself on a stage skill he cannot claim, and a great voice, at its best useful for the city when an honest man exploits it, does not excuse treachery. He gives these points considerable space in the peroration of *On the Dishonest Embassy* (19.337–339):

καίτοι καὶ περὶ τῆς φωνῆς ἴσως εἰπεῖν ἀνάγκη· πάνυ γὰρ μέγα καὶ
ἐπὶ ταύτῃ φρονεῖν αὐτὸν ἀκούω, ὡς καθυποκρινούμενον ὑμᾶς. ἐμοὶ
δὲ δοκεῖτ᾽ ἀτοπώτατον ἁπάντων ἂν ποιῆσαι, εἰ, ὅτε μὲν τὰ Θυέστου
καὶ τῶν ἐπὶ Τροίᾳ κάκ᾽ ἠγωνίζετο, ἐξεβάλλετ᾽ αὐτὸν καὶ ἐξεσυρίττετ᾽
ἐκ τῶν θεάτρων καὶ μόνον οὐ κατελεύεθ᾽ οὕτως ὥστε τελευτῶντα
τοῦ τριταγωνιστεῖν ἀποστῆναι, ἐπειδὴ δ᾽ οὐκ ἐπὶ τῆς σκηνῆς, ἀλλ᾽
ἐν τοῖς κοινοῖς καὶ μεγίστοις τῆς πόλεως πράγμασι μυρί᾽ εἴργασται

---

[39] Faraone 1989:156 (magic a tactic of the rich as well as the poor), 157 ("cognitive and verbal faculties which are essential to success in the law courts"), 158 (importance of the tongue).

κακά, τηνικαῦθ᾽ ὡς καλὸν φθεγγομένῳ προσέχοιτε. μηδαμῶς·
μηδὲν ὑμεῖς ἀβέλτερον πάθητε, ἀλλὰ λογίζεσθ᾽ ὅτι δεῖ κήρυκα μὲν
ἂν δοκιμάζητε, εὔφωνον σκοπεῖν, πρεσβευτὴν δὲ καὶ τῶν κοινῶν
ἀξιοῦντά τι πράττειν δίκαιον καὶ φρόνημ᾽ ἔχονθ᾽ ὑπὲρ μὲν ὑμῶν
μέγα, πρὸς δ᾽ ὑμᾶς ἴσον, ὥσπερ ἐγὼ Φίλιππον μὲν οὐκ ἐθαύμασα,
τοὺς δ᾽ αἰχμαλώτους ἐθαύμασα, ἔσωσα, οὐδὲν ὑπεστειλάμην. οὗτος
δ᾽ ἐκείνου μὲν προύκαλινδεῖτο, τοὺς παιᾶνας ᾖδεν, ὑμῶν δ᾽ ὑπερορᾷ.
ἔτι τοίνυν ὅταν μὲν ἴδητε δεινότητ᾽ ἢ εὐφωνίαν ἤ τι τῶν ἄλλων
τῶν τοιούτων ἀγαθῶν ἐπὶ χρηστοῦ καὶ φιλοτίμου γεγενημένον
ἀνθρώπου, συγχαίρειν καὶ συνασκεῖν πάντας δεῖ· κοινὸν γὰρ ὑμῖν
πᾶσι τοῖς ἄλλοις τοῦτ᾽ ἀγαθὸν γίγνεται· ὅταν δ᾽ ἐπὶ δωροδόκου καὶ
πονηροῦ καὶ παντὸς ἥττονος λήμματος, ἀποκλείειν καὶ πικρῶς καὶ
ἐναντίως ἀκούειν, ὡς πονηρίᾳ δυνάμεως δόξαν εὑρομένη παρ᾽ ὑμῶν
ἐπὶ τὴν πόλιν ἐστίν.

In fact perhaps I need to add a word about his voice. I hear he takes
considerable pride in it and expects to overwhelm you with his
delivery. In my view, it would be the most peculiar behavior on your
part if, when he portrayed the sufferings of Thyestes and the heroes
of Troy, you stopped him by driving him noisily from the theater
and practically stoning him to the point where he gave up his career
playing bit parts, yet when he has wreaked such disaster not on
stage but upon the city's most important, communal interests, you
pay him heed because of his beautiful voice. Do not do it. Do not be
so foolish. Rather, consider this: when you examine candidates for
the office of herald, you must look for someone with a good voice,
but when you examine candidates to serve as envoy and to promote
the city's interests, you must look for someone who is honest, who
is really proud to represent your interests but is content to be your
equal – as indeed I did not respect Philip, but I did respect the prisoners of war and saved them, sparing no effort. But this man grov-
eled before Philip, sang paeans, and scorns you. In addition, when
you find cleverness or vocal brilliance or some similar distinction
in an honest and magnanimous person, you should all share in the
satisfaction and training, for it will be a common benefit to all the
rest of you, But when you find this quality in a corrupt and wicked
person, one who cannot resist any chance at gain, you should all
shut him out and listen to him with rancor and animosity, because

wickedness that has acquired in your eyes the status of authority is destructive to the city.

Aeschines' specific vocal characteristic, according to Demosthenes (18.127), was shouting, a delivery style inappropriate to forensic speech, and even, by implication, to the theater:

εἰ γὰρ Αἰακὸς ἢ Ῥαδάμανθυς ἢ Μίνως ἦν ὁ κατηγορῶν, ἀλλὰ μὴ σπερμολόγος, περίτριμμ' ἀγορᾶς, ὄλεθρος γραμματεύς, οὐκ ἂν αὐτὸν οἶμαι ταῦτ' εἰπεῖν οὐδ' ἂν οὕτως ἐπαχθεῖς λόγους πορίσασθαι, ὥσπερ ἐν τραγῳδίᾳ βοῶντα "ὦ γῆ καὶ ἥλιε καὶ ἀρετὴ" καὶ τὰ τοιαῦτα, καὶ πάλιν "σύνεσιν καὶ παιδείαν" ἐπικαλούμενον, "ᾗ τὰ καλὰ καὶ τὰ αἰσχρα διαγιγνώσκεται·" ταῦτα γὰρ δήπουθεν ἠκούετ' αὐτοῦ λέγοντος.

If the prosecutor were Aeacus or Rhadamanthys or Minos and not a sponger, a common scoundrel, or a damned clerk, I don't believe he would have spoken that way or produced such repulsive expressions, bellowing as if on the tragic stage, "O earth and sun and virtue," and such like, or appealing to "understanding and education, through which we distinguish noble from base."

Perhaps many in the audience agreed with Demosthenes' description of Aeschines' speech style, but Carey (2000:10) is probably right to remark that

the fact that Demosthenes feels the need to make the attack is revealing. The skills and qualities that had served Aeschines in the theater were of equal value in the Assembly. There is abundant evidence that Aeschines had an impressive speaking voice . . ., a fact that must have particularly unnerved Demosthenes, whose own vocal powers seem to have been limited.[40]

Demosthenes' attacks on Aeschines for transferring a (supposedly) poor dramatic style to the Assembly and courts might be seen as a special case; more likely it is an opportunistic exploitation of a general prejudice against a speech style both out of place in the courtroom and reminiscent of the idiôtai who resorted to shouting.

---

[40] Carey points out that his service as Clerk might have also fostered Aeschines' vocal abilities (9–10). For more details on Demosthenes' intricate dancing around on the matter of Aeschines' stage experience, see Easterling 1999:156–162.

Singing

To illustrate an Attic idiom, the use of 'sing' to mean "speak in vain," Photius (alpha 551) records a fragment from Aristophanes' *Farmers* (*Georgoi* fr. 101a K-A), a comic interchange that depends on the audience's recognizing a juror's taunt, "You're singing!" (Bers 1985:3):

> {A} καὶ τὰς δίκας οὖν ἔλεγον ᾄδοντες τότε;
> {B} νὴ Δία· φράσω δ᾽ ἐγὼ μέγα σοι τεκμήριον·
> ἔτι γὰρ λέγουσ᾽ οἱ πρεσβύτεροι καθημένοι,
> ὅταν κακῶς <τις> ἀπολογῆται τὴν δίκην,
> "ᾄδεις".

A: They used to *sing* their pleas then?

B: Yes, by Zeus. I'll give you powerful evidence: Sitting in judgment the older men still say, whenever a man does a poor job of defending himself, "You're singing!"

This joke might have been reinforced by the audience's recognition of a variance from normal speech intonations brought about by a speaker's high emotion. At its extreme, strong feelings could overwhelm the usual tonal ups and downs of Greek into what sounded like singing. Evidence for this phenomenon comes from Aristoxenus, whose fourth-century floruit makes him roughly contemporary with some of the later orators of the Canon. In his *Elements of Harmony* (14.12–15 da Rios) he speaks of singing as the sustaining of a pitch:

> τὴν μὲν οὖν συνεχῆ λογικὴν εἶναί φαμεν, διαλεγομένων γὰρ ἡμῶν οὕτως ἡ φωνὴ κινεῖται κατὰ τόπον ὥστε μηδαμοῦ δοκεῖν ἵστασθαι. κατὰ δὲ τὴν ἑτέραν ἣν ὀνομάζομεν διαστηματικὴν ἐναντίως πέφυκε γίγνεσθαι· ἀλλὰ γὰρ ἵστασθαί τε δοκεῖ καὶ πάντες τὸν τοῦτο φαινόμενον ποιεῖν οὐκέτι λέγειν φασὶν ἀλλ᾽ ᾄδειν. διόπερ ἐν τῷ διαλέγεσθαι φεύγομεν τὸ ἱστάναι τὴν φωνήν, ἂν μὴ διὰ πάθος ποτὲ εἰς τοιαύτην κίνησιν ἀναγκασθῶμεν ἐλθεῖν, ἐν δὲ τῷ μελῳδεῖν τοὐναντίον ποιοῦμεν, τὸ μὲν γὰρ συνεχὲς φεύγομεν, τὸ δ᾽ ἑστάναι τὴν φωνὴν ὡς μάλιστα διώκομεν.

We say that the continuous [movement of the voice] is conversational [*logikên*], since when we are conversing, the voice changes position, with the result that it never seems to stay in one place.

In the second sort of [movement], which we call moving by intervals, the opposite is the case; as the voice seems to stay in place, and everyone says that the person who seems to do this is no longer speaking, but singing. For this reason, in conversation we avoid the holding of a pitch, unless we are forced on occasion by emotion [διὰ πάθος] into this sort of motion, whereas in singing we do the opposite, that is, we avoid continuous changes of pitch and seek to maximize the holding of the voice, that is, at a constant pitch.

It seems probable to me that the effect Aristoxenus attributes to πάθος could easily overwhelm a speaker under stress and lead to a ludicrous effect, namely singing a plea. In one of the passages in Aristophanes' *Birds* that joke about Athenian litigiousness (39–41, cited in chapter 2), the Athenians are said to sing their whole lives "upon their *dikôn*," their law cases, on boughs of litigation, as it were.[41] The notion of their singing may not be *only* an invention appropriate to this play, with all its birds. It seems to me quite likely that it was easy for a speaker's voice to slip into something incongruously musical, not from a poorly suppressed desire to exhibit the beauty of his voice, but from emotion.

Stanford (1967:28) must be right in calling Aristoxenus' distinction "too rigid." Besides variation in routine speech, the practice of forensic delivery, whether amateur or professional, probably ranged over a spectrum, from the monotonous to the ludicrously songlike. Direct testimony on the point is scanty and mostly late. Theophrastus, roughly contemporary with Aristoxenus and also a student of Aristotle, is quoted by Plutarch as remarking that both orators and actors "subtly approach singing" when delivering, respectively, their epilogues and lamentations.[42] Aside from songlike pitch modulation, a speaker with a natural tenor speaking voice and uneven articulation had reason to fear the jurors' disdain, since a high and/or wavering voice was among a suite of traits identified as effeminate, at least in discussions of rhetoric in later antiquity.[43]

---

[41] The cicadas sing for only a month or two (see p. 16).

[42] *Quaestiones Convivales* ("Table Talk') 623a–b: καὶ τοὺς ῥήτορας ἐν τοῖς ἐπιλόγοις καὶ τοὺς ὑποκριτὰς ἐν τοῖς ὀδυρμοῖς ἀτρέμα τῷ μελῳδεῖν προσάγοντας ὁρῶμεν καὶ παρεντείνοντας τὴν φωνήν.

[43] Among the pertinent texts: [Aristotle] *Physiognomy* 806b. For discussion of these notions in the second century AD see Gleason 1990. For another collection of texts describing undesirable speech traits, not however clearly connected to public speaking, see Halliwell 1990:70–71. For an analogous preference in another culture for "low pitch, low volume, and a laconic slowness" see Irvine 1984.

In Aristophanes' *Knights*, the Paphlagonian (i.e. Cleon, himself a highly successful symbouleutic speaker) insults the Sausage Seller by giving what looks like a generic description of how a near-*idiôtês*, swollen by a minor dicanic success, prepares a speech:

εἴ που δικίδιον εἶπας εὖ κατὰ ξένου μετοίκου,
τὴν νύκτα θρυλῶν καὶ λαλῶν ἐν ταῖς ὁδοῖς σεαυτῷ,
ὕδωρ τε πίνων κἀπιδεικνὺς τοὺς φίλους τ' ἀνιῶν,
ᾤου δυνατὸς εἶναι λέγειν.

If, on some occasion, you succeeded in pleading a piddling lawsuit against a metic, talking away to yourself, on and on, in the streets at night, and drinking (*sc.* only) water … and boring your friends by trying your speech on them, you thought you were a real orator!

Knights 347–350 (trans. Dover 1968b:151)

This suggests a rehearsal that probably aimed at an exact or approximate memorization of the text.

Now, having a prepared text, whether in one's hand or memorized, did not guarantee smooth sailing in court. Alcidamas, despiser of written texts, describes what happens when a man accustomed to writing out his speeches needs to improvise:[44]

ὅταν γάρ τις ἐθισθῇ κατὰ μικρὸν ἐξεργάζεσθαι τοὺς λόγους καὶ μετ' ἀκριβείας καὶ ῥυθμοῦ τὰ ῥήματα συντιθέναι, καὶ βραδείᾳ τῇ τῆς διανοίας κινήσει χρώμενος ἐπιτελεῖν τὴν ἑρμηνείαν, ἀναγκαῖόν ἐστι τοῦτον, ὅταν εἰς τοὺς αὐτοσχεδιαστοὺς ἔλθῃ λόγους, ἐναντία πράσσοντα ταῖς συνηθείαις ἀπορίας καὶ θορύβου πλήρη τὴν γνώμην ἔχειν, καὶ πρὸς ἅπαντα μὲν δυσχεραίνειν, μηδὲν δὲ διαφέρειν τῶν ἰσχνοφώνων, οὐδέποτε δ' εὐλύτῳ τῇ τῆς ψυχῆς ἀγχινοίᾳ χρώμενον ὑγρῶς καὶ φιλανθρώπως μεταχειρίζεσθαι τοὺς λόγους.

For when someone has been accustomed to work out speeches in detail and to construct sentences paying attention to both precise wording and rhythm and put over his interpretation making use of a slow mental process, it is inevitable that whenever this man comes to extempore speeches, doing the opposite of what he is used to, he

---

[44] In the course of a trial, this might happen because a litigant has failed to anticipate his opponent's arguments or feels he must respond to jurors' heckling (Bers 1985:5 with n15).

should have a mind full of helplessness and panic and should be ill-at-ease with everything, in no way different from those with speech impediments, never using a free readiness of wit to execute his speeches with flexibility and in a way that people like.

Alcidamas *Concerning Written Speeches* 16 (trans. J. V. Muir 2001)

Rhythm and Hiatus

Prose rhythm and the avoidance of hiatus were much discussed by the ancients,[45] but I know of no evidence that faults in these two technical areas of composition were ever explicitly attributed to amateur speakers. Some cautious inferences bearing on the speech of *idiôtai* are, nevertheless, possible.

First a general point. Most Athenians who listened to public speech probably noticed the cultivation by professionals (or at least some of them) of a style with perceptible qualities of rhythm and a relative rarity of hiatus (an acoustic phenomenon the Greeks usually referred to as a σύγκρουσις φωνηέτων, "collision of vowels"), even if they were not capable of or interested in analyzing and discussing rhetorical technique. Aristophanes expected his audience to recognize Thrasymachus as a crafty speaker (fr. 198.8 K-A), perhaps even as a speaker fond of a certain rhythm (see Aristotle *Rhetoric* 1409a). By the middle of the fourth century, if not before, Athenians who in their own routine speech were accustomed to eliminate a potential hiatus by saying, for instance, οὐ τότε, but οὐκ ἐγώ, were probably aware that some professional, or professionally assisted, speakers took pains to buffer vowels that would otherwise complete a word to prevent a collision with a word-initial vowel.[46] An amateur needing to speak in court might perhaps try to follow logographic practice, but my guess is that he would more likely think of these professional elegancies as lying well beyond his reach.

A specific characteristic of Demosthenes' speech style might be an ad hoc and ad hominem solution to a severe case of a general problem, the avoidance of tribrachs, or three successive short syllables, normally – and misleadingly –

---

[45] For a compact history of these controversies see McCabe 1981:1–41.

[46] Since we cannot be sure whether the audience was meant to recall and laugh at Hegelochus' failure to elide the word or his false accentuation or both (see Daitz 1983), I will not adduce Aristophanes *Frogs* 303–304 to show sensitivity to the means by which a potential hiatus was averted.

referred to as Blass's Law.[47] Blass (1887–98:3.1:105) makes a categorical statement as to Demosthenes' motive:

> Der Grund dieser Meidung ist derselbe, welcher auch in der älteren Tragödie die Auflösung der Hebung im Trimeter möglichst beschränken liess: der Vers und die Rede bewahren so eine straffere und männlichere Haltung.

> The motive for this avoidance [of tribrachs] is the same as that which causes the greatest possible restriction on the resolution [of long syllables] in the trimeters of older tragedy: by this means verse and oratory maintain a stricter and more manly bearing.

Blass does not explain why no other Attic orator observed this stricture. I conjecture that Demosthenes experienced tribrachs as exacerbating the vocal and psychological difficulties that impeded his speechmaking (discussed earlier in this chapter), perhaps without being able to explain just why the enunciation of a series of short syllables worsened his anxiety and reduced his volume.[48] In principle, he might have allowed the usual frequency of tribrachs when writing for clients, but it would be natural for the habit of avoiding them to persist, especially if he was not himself aware of it.[49] It seems very unlikely that a hapless *idiôtês* who suffered the same vocal difficulties as challenged the young Demosthenes would think of and successfully implement the strategy that I am suggesting motivated the application of "Blass's law."

---

[47] McCabe 1981 remains the authoritative statement on this and closely related features, e.g. the treatment of naturally short syllables at the close of sentences; for a summary of his conclusions see the fifth chapter.

[48] He might have been happier with only single short syllables, or even speaking exclusively in *molossi*, but the former would make expression of thought inordinately difficult, and the latter would be ludicrous in the extreme.

[49] Perhaps Demosthenes found it easier to coach clients in their delivery if the composition accommodated his own weakness.

5

PERFORMANCE AS EVIDENCE

F AR FROM BEING A SMALL TOWN where everybody kept everybody else under continual surveillance, Attica was a large territory with a large population, and it would be exceptional for a juror to know the people involved in a trial, unless perhaps they lived in the same deme or had served together in the army. Hence the outcome of a trial often depended on what the jurors deduced about the litigants from their performances and those of their *synergoi* in court.[1] What the jurors wanted to know, I think, was often less which of the adversaries had the better case than which of them was the "better" Athenian. For men of that culture, better or worse was substantially a matter of behavior in public. What he did within his *oikia* (house) could in principle have relevance to what we can call the man's "social or *polis* personality,"[2] and private-sphere behavior was sometimes lauded or condemned in court (Roisman 2005:56, 58, 146, 202). Admittedly, the jurors probably supposed that in principle litigants were likely to behave the same way whether in a meeting of the Ecclesia, standing in the hoplite line, drinking with their friends, or dealing with their parents, but that assumption could not often guide the jurors to any particular conclusion. The interested parties – litigants and their co-speakers and witnesses – could hardly be trusted to tell the jury the truth, since they were bound to tell very different stories. Moreover, there could be contradictions between what was most valued in public and private (Dover 1974:301–304).

---

[1] It seems self-evident that jurors would not very often separate their judgment of the litigants and their associates. "Guilt [or more rarely, innocence] by association" is the principle announced by a character at Euripides fr. 812.7–9: ὅστις δ' ὁμιλῶν ἥδεται κακοῖς ἀνήρ, / οὐ πώποτ' ἠρώτησα, γιγνώσκων ὅτι / τοιοῦτός ἐστιν οἷσπερ ἥδεται ξυνών ("I have never asked what sort of man takes pleasure in the company of evil men, since I know that a man shares the character of those whose company he enjoys"). Time limits are probably the main reason why fewer *synêgoroi*, most of whom would be men whose company a litigant enjoyed, are attested in private than in public suits: see Rubinstein 2000:65–70.

[2] I am deliberately avoiding the Greek term ἦθος, since it is sometimes understood (wrongly, in my opinion) as referring to an individual's personality: see Dover 1968b:76–77.

A citizen's performance in a civic space, before the eyes and ears of those who were to judge him, could, however, serve as a synecdoche for his qualities as a *politês*. What the jurors saw and heard for themselves, immediately before they cast their ballots, could be construed as the totality of what they needed to know about the litigants to reach a verdict.

I propose that two related aspects of social personality carried great weight in the courts: the litigants' willingness and ability to acknowledge the occasion as requiring a certain etiquette; and the litigants' relative mastery of their own emotions under the stress of the trial. Athenian litigiousness is generally treated by our sources as ridiculous or outrageous, but the persistence of the system must attest to its giving the Athenians a great measure of satisfaction (see Christ 1998 passim). One element of its success, obviously enough, was the replacement of disruptive acts of self-help by orderly process. Those litigants who most clearly signaled a respect for the civic order, not only by claiming that they did not habitually get into conflicts that required litigation, and that they were positively good citizens in their execution of military service and liturgies, but also by assimilating their self-presentation to the orderliness of the system and exhibiting an implicit confidence in the system, gained a greater measure of the jurors' good will than those who spoke with relatively greater show of affect.

It did not have to be this way. In some circumstances, unregulated emotion can be taken as an index of authenticity of feeling, and hence of the truth. Theophrastus reports that "in some places they . . . put fetters on the defendant [τῷ κρινομένῳ], as they say [is the practice] in Epizephyrian Locri. In situations of this kind, the culprits should generally be put into a state of emotional distress [εἰς ψυχίαν τε καὶ πάθος], as in instances of delay and in those matters which, when protracted, are harmful to the constitution" (*De eligendis magistratibus* Aly 56–63; trans. Keaney 1974:192). It is far from clear whether Theophrastus is describing a procedure whose general aims much resembled the adversary procedure of the Athenian courts or one that was just a form of extended humiliation and punishment; but it does seem likely that the Locrians regarded the defendants' distress (physical and psychological) as promoting their candor, perhaps even producing a confession. The rationale would, in that case, resemble the justification for exacting slave testimony under torture. Here, discomfiture applied by the procedure is seen as instrumental, and affect can be diagnostic.

But classical Athens seems in this respect to resemble the traditional culture of the Barotse [Lozi] people of Zambia, a litigious people indeed according to the ethnologist Max Gluckman, who writes that "[e]ven the most equable Lozi seems to be involved constantly in lawsuits" (1973:429). He reports: "The judges may be influenced, both in assessing evidence and in forming a conclusion on the merits of the case, by the manner in which the parties have respectively observed codes of etiquette or conformed to the ritual prescriptions and other customary modes of behavior" (Gluckman 1965:17). "Wrongdoers become angry in court to cover their wrongs. . . . However righteously indignant a man may be at a trespass on his rights, he should be calm in court, confident that the judges will see that justice is done" (Gluckman 1965:123).[3] Aside from testimony taken under torture, even if this was a real practice and not just a rhetorical *topos* (see Gagarin 1996), the Athenian courts were in this respect operating far more like Barotse tribunals two millennia later than contemporary courts in Epizephyrian Locri. It seems very likely that in Athenian courts the relevant codes of etiquette included the etiquette of the court itself.[4]

The second aspect of social personality emerges from generalizing the favored courtroom deportment, so that it becomes an index of the man's character. If a man can maintain his composure and dignity in the difficult circumstances of a trial, the jurors would tend to suppose not that this was a posture adopted ad hoc, put on like the three-piece suits adolescent boys on trial in American courts are advised to wear,[5] but an enduring set of related characteristics that manifest themselves as self-control or self-possession under stress (*egkrateia*) and orderliness (*eukosmia*). Several exemplary studies have canvassed aspects of this virtue and concepts closely related to it. I single out Helen North's *Sophrosyne* (1966), a classic study of self-control, and Joseph Roisman's *The Rhetoric of Manhood* (2005), which centers on the orators. These studies focus on explicit ideology, directly expressed claims and opinions. Roisman writes, "[I]t paid to convey the impression of being in possession of

---

[3] One might suppose that this preference for a calm presentation is not exclusively indigenous, but reflects also the influence of the colonial administration – that it is more British than Barotse. Gluckman, however, emphatically asserts that what he observed was deeply rooted in the native culture (1965:33) and the proceedings of British courts are "alien and often incomprehensible" to the Barotse. See also Gluckman 1973:246–252.

[4] Not that Athens was in this respect different from all other Greek states. *POxy* 410, a rhetorical treatise written in Doric, and therefore surely not meant in the first instance for the Athenian market, advises the reader to "take no pleasure in making indecorous or insolent statements, for that is mean and a sign of intemperate disposition, while the avoidance of abuse is a mark of high-mindedness and an ornament of speech" (col. 2.71–79, trans. Grenfell and Hunt). There are holes in the papyrus, but the earlier part (col. 1.11–12) specifies an audience of jurors.

[5] A New Haven, Connecticut, attorney, very experienced in the defense of such clients, has confirmed my layman's observation of this practice.

71

self-control and moderation, especially in the jury courts."[6] This observation is followed by examples in which speakers express attitudes and claim to have performed various acts in conformity with these values. In contrast, my principal business here is mainly to identify and analyze devices whereby speakers seek by implication to demonstrate that they are ἐγκρατεῖς and to undermine the appearance or reality of their opponents' ἐγκράτεια.

To my knowledge, no forensic speech claims in so many words that a man is exactly as he talks, but several other ancient texts come very close indeed. In anticipation, as it were, of Buffon's "*le style*, c'est l'homme même," Plato has Socrates say that the manner of a man's style and his speech correspond with his character (*êthos*).[7] The passages that come closest to identifying a trial as an event serving as a synecdoche appear in Dionysius of Halicarnassus' essay on Lysias (*Lysias* 8.8–15). In the first of these, the fundamental word is *eikones* (images or likenesses):[8]

οὐ γὰρ διανοουμένους μόνον ὑποτίθεται χρηστὰ καὶ ἐπιεικῆ καὶ μέτρια τοὺς λέγοντας, ὥστε εἰκόνας εἶναι δοκεῖν τῶν ἠθῶν τοὺς λόγους, ἀλλὰ καὶ τὴν λέξιν ἀποδίδωσι τοῖς ἤθεσιν οἰκείαν...

> Not only does Lysias present the speakers as men whose thoughts are honest, fair-minded, and moderate, with the result that their words seem to be images of their good characters, but he also gives them speech [or "speech style"] appropriate to their [good] characters . . .

In the second (*Lysias* 19.14–23), Dionysius is frank in acknowledging that Lysias uses language to compensate for his clients' shortcomings; moreover, the appearance of emotional control is among Lysias' strategies:

ὅταν δὲ μηδεμίαν ἀφορμὴν τοιαύτην λάβῃ παρὰ τῶν πραγμάτων, αὐτὸς ἠθοποιεῖ καὶ κατασκευάζει τὰ πρόσωπα τῷ λόγῳ πιστὰ καὶ

---

[6] Roisman 2005, esp. 178; cf. 198 for examples of the imputing of disorderly acts to one's opponents.

[7] *Republic* 400d: τί δ' ὁ πρόπος τῆς λέξεως, ἦν δ' ἐγώ, καὶ ὁ λόγος; οὐ τῷ τῆς ψυχῆς ἤθειἕπεται; πῶς γὰρ οὔ; ("What about the manner of speech, I said, and discourse? Does it not conform to the character of the soul? [Socrates' interlocutor answers] Certainly!"). Cf. Menander fr. 407: τί οὖν ἑτέρους λαλοῦντας εὖ βδελύττομαι; | τρόπος ἔσθ' ὁ πείθων τοῦ λέγοντος, οὐ λόγος. ("Why do I detest other men, the ones skilled at jabbering? Because it's the style that persuades, not the argument.") On Buffon's aphorism elegantly applied to historiography, see Gay 1974. For a perceptive survey of style in literary representation from epic to the fourth century, see Worman 2002.

[8] The passage is adduced by Dover (1968b:76–77).

χρηστά, προαιρέσεις τε αὐτοῖς ἀστείας ὑποτιθεὶς καὶ πάθη μέτρια προσάπτων καὶ λόγους ἐπιεικεῖς ἀποδιδούς ...

And when the facts fail to provide him with such material [i.e. that would indicate the speaker's worthy background and character], he creates his own moral tone, making his characters seem by their speech to be trustworthy and honest. He credits them with civilized dispositions and attributes controlled feelings to them and reasonable words ...

(Trans. Usher, adapted)[9]

Dionysius is, I believe, correct in identifying the effect Lysias strives to achieve, a self-presentation "spun" to make the client seem to be the sort of man who deals with his fellow citizens in a calm and fair-minded way. But I think Dionysius failed to understand the range of linguistic means by which the *logographos* helped his clients project that image.[10] The first passage continues as follows:

[λέξις] ἧ πέφυκεν αὐτὰ ἑαυτῶν κράτιστα δηλοῦσθαι, τὴν σαφῆ καὶ κυρίαν καὶ κοινὴν καὶ πᾶσιν ἀνθρώποις συνηθεστάτην· ὁ γὰρ ὄγκος καὶ τὸ ξένον καὶ τὸ ἐξ ἐπιτηδεύσεως ἅπαν ἀνηθοποίητον. καὶ συντίθησί γε αὐτὴν ἀφελῶς πάνυ καὶ ἁπλῶς, ὁρῶν ὅτι οὐκ ἐν τῇ περιόδῳ καὶ τοῖς ῥυθμοῖς, ἀλλ' ἐν τῇ διαλελυμένῃ λέξει γίνεται τὸ ἦθος.

... by its nature [style] displays them in their best light – clear, standard, ordinary speech which is thoroughly familiar to everyone. All forms of pompous, outlandish, and contrived language are foreign to characterization. As to his composition, it is absolutely simple and straightforward. He sees that characterization is achieved not by periodic structure and the use of rhythms, but by loosely connected sentences.

(*Lysias* 8.11–21; trans. Usher)

---

[9] A short lyric poem, *PMG* 889, expresses the wish that one could split open a man's chest and look inside. Cf. Euripides *Medea* 516–519 and *Hippolytus* 925–927. One might say that performance in court was a *pis aller* for that sort of exploratory surgery.

[10] It may seem impertinent for a modern to criticize the linguistic discernment of a native speaker of Greek who lived only a few centuries after the authors he discusses, but I am hardly the first to do so; see, for instance, Macleod's criticism of Dionysius' analysis of Thucydidean style (1979).

In speaking only of the advantages of adhering to familiar language, Dionysius (*Lysias* 8.21–34) elides the differences between even the simplest forms of literary prose and colloquial speech; or rather, he claims that the simplicity of Lysianic prose is in fact a deception of extraordinary skill:

δοκεῖ μὲν γὰρ ἀποίητός τις εἶναι καὶ ἀτεχνίτευτος ὁ τῆς ἁρμονίας αὐτοῦ χαρακτὴρ καὶ οὐ θαυμάσαιμ' ἄν, εἰ πᾶσι μὲν τοῖς ἰδιώταις, οὐκ ὀλίγοις δὲ καὶ τῶν φιλολόγων, ὅσοι μὴ μεγάλας ἔχουσι τριβὰς περὶ λόγους, τοιαύτην τινὰ παράσχοι δόξαν, ὅτι ἀνεπιτηδεύτως καὶ οὐ κατὰ τέχνην, αὐτομάτως δέ πως καὶ ὡς ἔτυχε σύγκειται. ἔστι δὲ παντὸς μᾶλλον ἔργου τεχνικοῦ κατεσκευασμένος. πεποίηται γὰρ αὐτῷ τοῦτο τὸ ἀποίητον καὶ δέδεται τὸ λελυμένον καὶ ἐν αὐτῷ τῷ μὴ δοκεῖν δεινῶς κατεσκευάσθαι τὸ δεινὸν ἔχει. τὴν ἀλήθειαν οὖν τις ἐπιτηδεύων καὶ φύσεως μιμητὴς γίνεσθαι βουλόμενος οὐκ ἂν ἁμαρτάνοι τῇ Λυσίου συνθέσει χρώμενος· ἑτέραν γὰρ οὐκ ἂν εὕροι ταύτης ἀληθεστέραν.

As a further general comment on this quality, I may say that I do not know of any other orator – at least any who employs a similar sentence-structure – with greater charm or persuasiveness. The distinctive nature of its melodious composition seems, as it were, not to be contrived or formed by any conscious art, and it would not surprise me if every layman, and even many of those scholars who have not specialized in oratory, should receive the impression that this arrangement has not been deliberately and artistically devised, but is somehow spontaneous and fortuitous. Yet it is more carefully composed than any work of art. For this artlessness is itself the product of art: the relaxed structure is really under control, and it is in the very illusion of not having been composed with masterly skill that the mastery lies. Therefore the student of realism and naturalism would not go wrong if he were to follow Lysias in his composition, for he will find no model who is more true to life.

(Trans. Usher)

And yet Dionysius does not often show just how Lysias executed his masterpieces of covert artfulness. Modern scholars, perhaps because they learned classical Greek as a dead language, solely by the artificial means available to anyone born long after the death of its last native speakers, have managed to discover at least a few of the tricks Dionysius could only intuit in what was for him already a classical text.[11]

Like "manhood," ἐγκράτεια is not a precisely demarcated set of qualities or actions.[12] Differences in occasion and degree can easily throw any simplification off the tracks, and paradoxes abound. In a passage of Demosthenes 53 discussed by Roisman (2005:54), Apollodorus, who delivered and most probably wrote the speech, feels no risk in reporting his own distress at the plight of a friend who has been kidnapped; the primary sufferer was not himself but his friend, and Apollodorus himself certainly does not interrupt his speech to fetch a sigh in recollection of his own emotion.[13] As Roisman argues in his discussion of Demosthenes' prosecution of Meidias (2005:76–77), a man's decision to litigate rather than settle the issue by physical violence could make the virtue I am calling ἐγκράτεια an effective excuse for failing to do what would ordinarily be regarded as the "manly thing." Expectations based on stereotypes were in play, particularly in the matter of the litigants' ages, a topic often addressed in surviving speeches and contemporary discursive texts. Most often cited is Lysias 16, a speech delivered by a young man in a very tight spot indeed.[14] The speaker opens with an arrogant boast (16.2):

ἐγὼ γὰρ οὕτω σφόδρα ἐμαυτῷ πιστεύω, ὥστ' ἐλπίζω καὶ εἴ τις πρός με τυγχάνει ἀηδῶς [ἢ κακῶς] διακείμενος.

I am so utterly confident in myself that I expect even someone badly disposed towards me to change his mind when he hears me speak about what happened and to think much better of me in the future.

[11] Immediately pertinent to this discussion is what Dover 1968b:83–86 analyzes soon after discussing Dionysius' remarks on Lysias' style: the means by which speakers in Lysias signal the progression of events in their narratives. To my knowledge, the phenomenon was not noticed until Fraenkel 1962.

[12] "[M]anhood ... was an all-encompassing perception that the Athenians were happy to leave ill defined. ... The concept is too complex and full of contradictions, most likely because the 'practitioners of masculinity' – the investigator's human subjects – often fail to agree about what it entails, or what makes a manly man" (Roisman 2005:2). The description of a man as ἀπράγμων (not officious or meddlesome) was particularly susceptible to being "spun" as either a compliment or an insult: Roisman 2005:182.

[13] See also Roisman 2005:97 for a discussion of the celebrated "open texture" passage at Demosthenes 22.25–27. Hyperides might be said to minimize the paradox by drawing a distinction between, on the one hand, manliness combined with rational reflection and, on the other, thoughtless and emotional audacity: see Roisman 2005:111.

[14] The speech was for delivery by one Mantitheus, who had served the Thirty Tyrants, at a *dokimasia* conducted by the restored democracy.

He soon plays on the very prejudice exemplified by that claim to his own advantage (16.11):

περὶ δὲ τῶν κοινῶν μοι μέγιστον ἡγοῦμαι τεκμήριον εἶναι τῆς ἐμῆς ἐπιεικείας, ὅτι τῶν νεωτέρων ὅσοι περὶ κύβους ἢ πότους ἢ τὰς τοιαύτας ἀκολασίας τυγχάνουσι τὰς διατριβὰς ποιούμενοι, πάντας αὐτοὺς ὄψεσθέ μοι διαφόρους ὄντας καίτοι δῆλον ὅτι, εἰ τῶν αὐτῶν ἐπεθυμοῦμεν, οὐκ ἂν τοιαύτην γνώμην εἶχον περὶ ἐμοῦ.

As far as public life is concerned, I believe the strongest proof of my good conduct is this: you will see that those of the young men who spend their time playing dice, drinking, and participating in that sort of unruliness are all hostile to me. . . . It is clear that they would not take that attitude towards me if we had the same interests.[15]

This view of young men is adduced as early as Antiphon *Tetralogy* 3.3.2[16] and continues to be expressed, sometimes quite luridly, through the fourth century.

[15] Similarly, §19 runs against the grain in a plea not to rely on surface manifestations of character, including "reticence and a decorous style of [*kosmiôs* – the adverb related to *kosmos*] dress": ὥστε οὐκ ἄξιον ἀπ' ὄψεως, ὦ βουλή, οὔτε φιλεῖν οὔτε μισεῖν οὐδένα, ἀλλ' ἐκ τῶν ἔργων σκοπεῖν· πολλοὶ μὲν γὰρ μικρὸν διαλεγόμενοι καὶ κοσμίως ἀμπεχόμενοι μεγάλων κακῶν αἴτιοι γεγόνασιν, ἕτεροι δὲ τῶν τοιούτων ἀμελοῦντες πολλὰ κἀγαθὰ ὑμᾶς εἰσιν εἰργασμένοι.

[16] μάθετε δὴ πρῶτον μὲν ὅτι ἄρξαι καὶ παροινεῖν τοὺς νεωτέρους τῶν πρεσβυτέρων εἰκότερόν ἐστι· τοὺς μὲν γὰρ ἥ τε μεγαλοφροσύνη τοῦ γένους ἥ τε ἀκμὴ τῆς ῥώμης ἥ τε ἀπειρία τῆς μέθης ἐπαίρει τῷ θυμῷ χαρίζεσθαι, τοὺς δὲ ἥ τε ἐμπειρία τῶν παροινουμένων ἥ τε ἀσθένεια τοῦ γήρως ἥ τε δύναμις τῶν νέων φοβοῦσα σωφρονίζει. (". . . you know that young men are more likely [*eikos*] to get drunk and start a fight than old men; for they are proud of their age [others understand "social rank of the family into which they were born"] at their peak physically, and not used to drinking, all of which arouse their anger. Old men, however, tend to control themselves, since they are used to drinking, are weak in old age, and fear the strength of the young.")

Those who speak for the defendant, who has evidently availed himself of his right to withdraw from Attica before the jury votes, try to disarm the age stereotype at *Tetralogy* 3.4.2 by observing that "many young men act with restraint, and many of the elderly become violent when drunk, so this argument does not support the prosecutor any more than the defendant." For discussion of age stereotypes see, *inter alia*, Dover 1974:102–106 and Roisman 2005:11–25.

6

APPEALS TO PITY AND DISPLAYS OF ANGER

Appealing to Pity

SEVERAL VERY WELL-KNOWN DESCRIPTIONS of court speakers and actual passages of court speech have lead many scholars to conclude that litigants wallowed in emotion as they made appeals to the jury's pity (in older terminology, appeals *ad misericordiam*). This might have been true of many amateurs, but very seldom, as I see it, of the professionals.

A locus classicus is Socrates' declaration, as represented by Plato at *Apology* 34d3–35b8, that he will not demean himself or his city by carrying on in the contemptible manner he has often witnessed:[1]

> εἶεν δή, ὦ ἄνδρες· ἃ μὲν ἐγὼ ἔχοιμ' ἂν ἀπολογεῖσθαι, σχεδόν ἐστι ταῦτα καὶ ἄλλα ἴσως τοιαῦτα. τάχα δ' ἄν τις ὑμῶν ἀγανακτήσειεν ἀναμνησθεὶς ἑαυτοῦ, εἰ ὁ μὲν καὶ ἐλάττω τουτουΐ τοῦ ἀγῶνος ἀγῶνα ἀγωνιζόμενος ἐδεήθη τε καὶ ἱκέτευσε τοὺς δικαστὰς μετὰ πολλῶν δακρύων, παιδία τε αὐτοῦ ἀναβιβασάμενος ἵνα ὅτι μάλιστα ἐλεηθείη, καὶ ἄλλους τῶν οἰκείων καὶ φίλων πολλούς, ἐγὼ δὲ οὐδὲν ἄρα τούτων ποιήσω, καὶ ταῦτα κινδυνεύων, ὡς ἂν δόξαιμι, τὸν ἔσχατον κίνδυνον. τάχ' ἂν οὖν τις ταῦτα ἐννοήσας αὐθαδέστερον ἂν πρός με σχοίη καὶ ὀργισθεὶς αὐτοῖς τούτοις θεῖτο ἂν μετ' ὀργῆς τὴν ψῆφον. εἰ δή τις ὑμῶν οὕτως ἔχει – οὐκ ἀξιῶ μὲν γὰρ ἔγωγε, εἰ δ' οὖν – ἐπιεικῆ ἄν μοι δοκῶ πρὸς τοῦτον λέγειν λέγων ὅτι "ἐμοί, ὦ ἄριστε, εἰσὶν μέν πού τινες καὶ οἰκεῖοι· καὶ γὰρ τοῦτο αὐτὸ τὸ

---

[1] Plato here represents Socrates as acknowledging frequent attendance at court sessions (34a4: ἐγὼ πολλάκις ἑώρακά τινας ὅταν κρίνωνται ["I have often seen certain men, when on trial . . ."]). This statement confirms Burnet's interpretation of *Apology* 17d.2, νῦν ἐγὼ πρῶτον ἐπὶ δικαστήριον ἀναβέβηκα ("now for the first time I am appearing before a court"): "All he says is that he has never appeared as a party to a case."

τοῦ Ὁμήρου, οὐδ' ἐγὼ 'ἀπὸ δρυὸς οὐδ' ἀπὸ πέτρης' πέφυκα ἀλλ' ἐξ
ἀνθρώπων, ὥστε καὶ οἰκεῖοί μοί εἰσι καὶ ὑεῖς γε, ὦ ἄνδρες Ἀθηναῖοι,
τρεῖς, εἷς μὲν μειράκιον ἤδη, δύο δὲ παιδία· ἀλλ' ὅμως οὐδένα αὐτῶν
δεῦρο ἀναβιβασάμενος δεήσομαι ὑμῶν ἀποψηφίσασθαι." τί δὴ οὖν
οὐδὲν τούτων ποιήσω; οὐκ αὐθαδιζόμενος, ὦ ἄνδρες Ἀθηναῖοι, οὐδ'
ὑμᾶς ἀτιμάζων, ἀλλ' εἰ μὲν θαρραλέως ἐγὼ ἔχω πρὸς θάνατον ἢ μή,
ἄλλος λόγος, πρὸς δ' οὖν δόξαν καὶ ἐμοὶ καὶ ὑμῖν καὶ ὅλῃ τῇ πόλει οὐ
μοι δοκεῖ καλὸν εἶναι ἐμὲ τούτων οὐδὲν ποιεῖν καὶ τηλικόνδε ὄντα
καὶ τοῦτο τοὔνομα ἔχοντα, εἴτ' οὖν ἀληθὲς εἴτ' οὖν ψεῦδος, ἀλλ' οὖν
δεδογμένον γέ ἐστί τῳ Σωκράτη διαφέρειν τῶν πολλῶν ἀνθρώπων.
εἰ οὖν ὑμῶν οἱ δοκοῦντες διαφέρειν εἴτε σοφίᾳ εἴτε ἀνδρείᾳ εἴτε
ἄλλῃ ἡτινιοῦν ἀρετῇ τοιοῦτοι ἔσονται, αἰσχρὸν ἂν εἴη· οἵουσπερ
ἐγὼ πολλάκις ἑώρακά τινας ὅταν κρίνωνται, δοκοῦντας μέν τι
εἶναι, θαυμάσια δὲ ἐργαζομένους, ὡς δεινόν τι οἰομένους πείσεσθαι
εἰ ἀποθανοῦνται, ὥσπερ ἀθανάτων ἐσομένων ἂν ὑμεῖς αὐτοὺς μὴ
ἀποκτείνητε· οἳ ἐμοὶ δοκοῦσιν αἰσχύνην τῇ πόλει περιάπτειν, ὥστ'
ἄν τινα καὶ τῶν ξένων ὑπολαβεῖν ὅτι οἱ διαφέροντες Ἀθηναίων εἰς
ἀρετήν, οὓς αὐτοὶ ἑαυτῶν ἔν τε ταῖς ἀρχαῖς καὶ ταῖς ἄλλαις τιμαῖς
προκρίνουσιν, οὗτοι γυναικῶν οὐδὲν διαφέρουσιν. ταῦτα γάρ, ὦ
ἄνδρες Ἀθηναῖοι, οὔτε ὑμᾶς χρὴ ποιεῖν τοὺς δοκοῦντας καὶ ὁπηοῦν
τι εἶναι, οὔτ', ἂν ἡμεῖς ποιῶμεν, ὑμᾶς ἐπιτρέπειν, ἀλλὰ τοῦτο αὐτὸ
ἐνδείκνυσθαι, ὅτι πολὺ μᾶλλον καταψηφιεῖσθε τοῦ τὰ ἐλεινὰ ταῦτα
δράματα εἰσάγοντος καὶ καταγέλαστον τὴν πόλιν ποιοῦντος ἢ τοῦ
ἡσυχίαν ἄγοντος.

Well, that, and things just about like it, is what I have to say in my
defense. Some one of you might be irked, remembering his own
actions, if on trial for something less momentous, he asked and
beseeched the jurors, weeping copiously, and marching his children
up here to win as much pity as he could, and also many other relatives and friends, but I do none of that; and, on top of that, though
I am – so it might seem – facing the most extreme danger. Some of
you might, on thinking about it, adopt the harshest attitude to me,
and growing angry for this reason, cast your votes in anger. If any of
you is feeling that way – I don't think it would be right, but just in
case – I think it would be proper for me to answer him like this: "Sir,
I do have, I think, some family; you see, it's like that bit in Homer, 'I
don't come from oak or rock, but from human beings,' so I do have
family, sons actually, men of Athens, three of them, one already a

young man, and two children. Still, I am not going to get any of them to come up here, and I will not beg you to acquit me." Why won't I do any of these things? Not out of arrogance, gentlemen of Athens, and not to show you lack of respect. If I do or don't feel confident about death – well, that's another story. But as for reputation, my own, yours, the whole city's, it does not seem noble for me to do any of that, especially at my age and having the name I do: whether it is true or false, it is a matter of fixed belief that Socrates is, in some way, beyond most men. So if those of you who suppose that they have some reputation for wisdom or manliness or some other point of excellence carried on in this manner, it would be shameful. I have often see men in this category, men who seemed to be of some value, behaving in an *amazing* fashion, in the belief that they were going to suffer something terrible if they died, as if they would live forever if only you did not execute them. These men seem to hang a badge of shame around the city's neck, with the consequence that a foreigner would suppose that Athenians preeminent for their virtue, men whom the Athenians prefer to themselves in assigning official positions and other honors – that these men were no better than women. Gentlemen of Athens, neither should you who pride yourselves on being of some value do this, nor should we allow you to; rather, you should make this clear: you are more likely to convict the man who brings in these piteous dramas and makes the city a laughingstock than the man who keeps his peace.

The sarcastic phrases θαυμάσια δὲ ἐργαζομένους ("behaving in an *amazing* fashion"), οὗτοι γυναικῶν οὐδὲν διαφέρουσιν ("these men are no better than women"), and τὰ ἐλεινὰ ταῦτα δράματα ("these piteous dramas") are remarkable for the utter lack of compassion and forbearance they manifest. But as reportage, Plato might provide an accurate description of the appeal to pity as it was performed by a speaker facing the possibility of execution, or even lesser punishments, if he failed to win his case.[2]

---

[2] Unsurprisingly, a much older Plato retained his contempt for "shameful supplications and effeminate lamentations" and would empower the judges to interrupt these and other utterances he regarded as unsuitable, including oaths (*Laws* 949b). Apropos the accuracy of Socrates' charge, one might compare the claim, unsubstantiated in its specifics, in the *Protagoras* about the shouting down of men on the *bêma* (319b–c). Plato was of course eager to heroize Socrates, and that desire, together with his own disgust for the democratic courts, might explain the discrepancy between him and Xenophon, who actually calls such appeals during an *antitimêsis* illegal: see Konstan 2001:36.

We meet the best known among comic descriptions of these appeals in Aristophanes' *Wasps*, in Philocleon's ecstatic description of the joys of jury service.[3] Supplications begin outside the court:

καὶ μὴν εὐθύς γ' ἀπὸ βαλβίδων περὶ τῆς ἀρχῆς ἀποδείξω
τῆς ἡμετέρας ὡς οὐδεμιᾶς ἥττων ἐστὶν βασιλείας.
τί γὰρ εὔδαιμον καὶ μακαριστὸν μᾶλλον νῦν ἐστι δικαστοῦ,
ἢ τρυφερώτερον ἢ δεινότερον ζῷον, καὶ ταῦτα γέροντος;
ὃν πρῶτα μὲν ἕρποντ' ἐξ εὐνῆς τηροῦσ' ἐπὶ τοῖσι δρυφάκτοις
ἄνδρες μεγάλοι καὶ τετραπήχεις· κἄπειτ' εὐθὺς προσιόντι
ἐμβάλλει μοι τὴν χεῖρ' ἁπαλὴν τῶν δημοσίων κεκλοφυῖαν.
ἱκετεύουσίν θ' ὑποκύπτοντες τὴν φωνὴν οἰκτροχοοῦντες·
"οἴκτιρόν μ', ὦ πάτερ, αἰτοῦμαί σ', εἰ καὐτὸς πώποθ' ὑφείλου
ἀρχὴν ἄρξας ἢ 'πὶ στρατιᾶς τοῖς ξυσσίτοις ἀγοράζων."
ὃς ἔμ' οὐδ' ἂν ζῶντ' ᾔδειν, εἰ μὴ διὰ τὴν προτέραν ἀπόφυξιν.

I will show you, beginning at the startling-line, how our power is second to no monarchical rule. These days, what living thing is happier and more blessed than a juryman or more pampered or more awe-inspiring? – and I'm talking about an old man! First off, when I creep out of bed they're looking for me at the courtroom railing – big, six-foot men. And then, right away, as soon as I come near, he [the defendant] puts out his hand, his hand soft from filching from the public till instead of working. They kowtow and beg me, and pour out a miserable lament: "Pity me, sir, I beg you, if you ever kept something back for yourself when serving in an office or on campaign when you shopped for your messmates." This is somebody who wouldn't have even known I was alive, if it weren't for an acquittal once before.

Wasps 548–558

And piteous entreaties, says Philocleon, continue within the trial itself as litigants bemoan their poverty and, should stories and jokes fail to please, culminate in the parading of children before the jury:

. . . τὰ παιδάρι' εὐθὺς ἀνέλκει
τὰς θηλείας καὶ τοὺς υἱεῖς τῆς χειρός, ἐγὼ δ' ἀκροῶμαι,
τὰ δὲ συγκύψανθ' ἅμα βληχᾶται, κἄπειθ' ὁ πατὴρ ὑπὲρ αὐτῶν
ὥσπερ θεὸν ἀντιβολεῖ με τρέμων τῆς εὐθύνης ἀπολῦσαι·

---

[3] See Johnstone 1999:174nn55–56 for discussion of whether jurors could be so approached in the fourth century.

"εἰ μὲν χαίρεις ἀρνὸς φωνῇ, παιδὸς φωνὴν ἐλεήσαις"
εἰ δ' αὖ τοῖς χοιριδίοις χαίρω, θυγατρὸς φωνῇ με πιθέσθαι.
χἠμεῖς αὐτῷ τότε τῆς ὀργῆς ὀλίγον τὸν κόλλοπ' ἀνεῖμεν.

Right away he leads his children up to the podium, girls and boys, taking them by the hand; and I listen, and they all bow and scrape *ensemble*; and then, on their behalf, their father, trembling, begs me, as if I were a god, to let him off at his *euthuna* [audit on leaving office]: "If you rejoice on hearing the voice of a lamb, take pity as you hear a boy's voice"; or if it's piglets that give me my jollies, he begs me to hearken to his daughter's voice. And then we crank down our anger for him.

Wasps 568–573

For a variety of reasons I believe we are again dealing with a sort of optical illusion. We must discriminate between accounts or predictions of these pleas as they are presented by a litigant's opponents or, as in the case of Plato and Aristophanes, writers with anti-democratic or comedic purposes. We cannot assume affective delivery within the courtroom on the basis of verbal similarities to appeals enacted outside of courts. We must recognize the function of these pleas in the overall framework of a lawcourt pleading. Above all, we must be alert to differences between professional and amateur speaking styles.

I have found very little useful for this investigation in the scraps that describe early rhetorical theory. An important exception is the evidence available for Thrasymachus of Chalcedon, a prominent figure among fifth-century theorists of rhetoric, who is reported to have devoted a work to *eleoi*, "Appeals for Pity." From brief mentions in Plato and Aristotle we know something – but not much – of its content. In his potted history of the *technê logôn* in the *Phaedrus* Socrates speaks of Thrasymachus as a master of piteous groans and techniques in the incitement, and subsequent calming, of the listeners' indignation:

τῶν γε μὴν οἰκτρογόων ἐπὶ γῆρας καὶ πενίαν ἑλκομένων λόγων
κεκρατηκέναι τέχνῃ μοι φαίνεται τὸ τοῦ Χαλκηδονίου σθένος,
ὀργίσαι τε αὖ πολλοὺς ἅμα δεινὸς ἀνὴρ γέγονεν, καὶ πάλιν
ὠργισμένοις ἐπᾴδων κηλεῖν, ὡς ἔφη·

The mighty Chalcedonian seems to me to be supreme in the realm of artfully extracting piteous, groaning arguments applicable to old age and poverty, and to have been cunning as well at rousing masses of men to anger and, once they were enraged, to beguiling them with charms, as he said.

Phaedrus 267c7–d4

The arch reference to Thrasymachus by means of a Homeric-sounding periphrasis, literally "the strength of Chalcedon," is probably a backhanded compliment to the power of the *eleos* performed according to his instruction.[4] Aristotle's disdain for the performative elements of oratory[5] presumably explains the brevity of his remarks on Thrasymachus:

διαφέρει γάρ τι πρὸς τὸ δηλῶσαι ὡδὶ ἢ ὡδὶ εἰπεῖν, οὐ μέντοι τοσοῦτον, ἀλλ᾽ ἅπαντα φαντασία ταῦτ᾽ ἐστί, καὶ πρὸς τὸν ἀκροατήν· διὸ οὐδεὶς οὕτω γεωμετρεῖν διδάσκει. ἐκείνη μὲν οὖν ὅταν ἔλθῃ ταὐτὸ ποιήσει τῇ ὑποκριτικῇ, ἐγκεχειρήκασιν δὲ ἐπ᾽ ὀλίγον περὶ αὐτῆς εἰπεῖν τινές, οἷον Θρασύμαχος ἐν τοῖς Ἐλέοις·

To speak in one way rather than another does make some difference in regard to clarity, though not a great difference; but all these things are forms of outward show and intended to affect the audience. As a result, nobody teaches geometry this way. Whenever delivery comes to be considered it will function in the same way as acting, and some have tried to say a little about it, for example, Thrasymachus in his [account of] emotional appeals.

Rhetoric 1404a10–18 (trans. Kennedy 1991)

---

[4] Thrasymachus' teaching might have consisted only in model speeches: see Cole 1991, chap. 5, esp. 83–84.

[5] Aristotle's meaning at *Rhetoric* 1401b3–9 is uncertain. The first underlined word carries an ambiguous connotation; the second is textually dubious:

ἄλλος δὲ τόπος τὸ <u>δεινώσει</u> κατασκευάζειν ἢ ἀνασκευάζειν· τοῦτο δ᾽ ἐστὶν ὅταν, μὴ δείξας ὅτι ἐποίησεν <μηδ᾽ ὅτι οὐκ ἐποίησεν>, αὐξήσῃ τὸ πρᾶγμα· ποιεῖ γὰρ φαίνεσθαι ἢ ὡς οὐ πεποίηκεν, ὅταν ὁ τὴν αἰτίαν ἔχων <u>ὀργίζηται</u>, ἢ ὡς πεποίηκεν, ὅταν ὁ κατηγορῶν αὐξῇ.

Kennedy's translation runs: "Another topic is constructing or demolishing an argument by *exaggeration*. This occurs when one amplifies the action without showing that it was performed; for when [the accused] amplifies the charge, he causes it to appear that he has not committed the action, or when the accuser *goes into a rage* [he makes it appear] that [the defendant] has." δείνωσις might possibly suggest treating some action as horrifying, and using voice and gesture to drive home the point, in which case the translation is too restrained. ὀργίζηται, on the other hand, for which Kennedy gives a full-blooded translation, is the reading of several manuscripts, but it was emended by W. D. Ross in his 1959 Oxford edition to αὐξῇ, "augment" or "exaggerate."

Aristotle was quick to turn up his nose at what went on in Athenian courts, but I conjecture that Thrasymachus' attention to this aspect of speechmaking shows that it was widely regarded as very important, and also as treacherous, and therefore not to be left to a speaker's instincts. If that is so, we have direct evidence for concentrated attention to the critical role of affect in speaker and audience.

The plangent style (discussed at further length later in this chapter) is both a "natural" mode and the particular speech style most often despised and ridiculed, as in the two passages cited at the opening of this section. Condemnations of appeals to pity certainly have evidentiary value for what went on in court pleadings, but they cannot be adduced *tout court* to demonstrate that the plangent style was an element in professional speech. They often predict what, in effect, they *hope* the speaker's opponents will do, or else they describe in a highly tendentious manner what the opponents have already done.[6] In fact, analysis of professionally composed appeals (especially by Konstan 2001) shows rather that they are formulaic, hence controlled, closely linked to defendants' factual claims, and often couched so as to pander to the jurors' self-interest in protecting patriotic men and their families.

Consider, for instance, the three instances of *ad misericordiam* appeals adduced by Burnet ad *Apology* 34c3. First, Lysias 20.34:

καίτοι ὁρῶ μέν γ' ὑμᾶς, ὦ ἄνδρες δικασταί, ἐάν τις παῖδας αὐτοῦ ἀναβιβασάμενος κλάῃ καὶ ὀλοφύρηται, τούς τε παῖδας δι' αὐτὸν εἰ ἀτιμωθήσονται ἐλεοῦντας, καὶ ἀφιέντας τὰς τῶν πατέρων ἁμαρτίας διὰ τοὺς παῖδας, οὓς οὔπω ἴστε εἴτε ἀγαθοὶ εἴτε κακοὶ ἡβήσαντες γενήσονται· ἡμᾶς δ' ἴστε ὅτι πρόθυμοι γεγενήμεθα εἰς ὑμᾶς, καὶ τὸν πατέρα οὐδὲν ἡμαρτηκότα. ὥστε πολλῷ δικαιότεροί ἐστε, ὧν πεπείρασθε, τούτοις χαρίσασθαι, ἢ οὓς οὐκ ἴστε ὁποῖοί τινες ἔσονται. πεπόνθαμεν δὲ τοὐναντίον τοῖς ἄλλοις ἀνθρώποις. οἱ μὲν γὰρ ἄλλοι τοὺς παῖδας παραστησάμενοι ἐξαιτοῦνται ὑμᾶς, ἡμεῖς δὲ τὸν πατέρα τουτονὶ καὶ ἡμᾶς ἐξαιτούμεθα, μὴ ἡμᾶς ἀντὶ μὲν ἐπιτίμων ἀτίμους ποιήσητε, ἀντὶ δὲ πολιτῶν ἀπόλιδας· ἀλλὰ ἐλεήσατε καὶ τὸν πατέρα γέροντα ὄντα καὶ ἡμᾶς.

Nevertheless, gentlemen of the jury, we see that if somebody brings forward his children and weeps and laments, you take pity on the children if they are to lose their citizen rights on his account, and

---

[6] Johnstone 1999:110: "a prosecutor's warning against what a defendant might do does not prove that he actually did it." Johnstone's analysis is discussed at further length later in this chapter.

you pardon the father's crimes on account of the children, without knowing whether they are going to turn out well or badly when they grow up. In our case, you know that we have been loyal to you and that our father has done nothing wrong. So it will be far more just for you to reward those whom you have tested, rather than people whose future development is unknown to you. Our predicament is the opposite of other people's: they bring forward their children and plead with you; we bring forward our father and ourselves, and beg you not to deprive us of citizen rights and of citizenship. Take pity on our father, who is an old man, and on us.

As part of an argument *a fortiori* (or perhaps question-begging), the speaker denies his father's guilt. This passage is remarkable for describing the jurors' pity as normally extended to the children put on display in spite of the father's guilt, and granted in anticipation of the children proving better than their father.[7] The appeal is made by an implicit *praeteritio*, as if the defendant's son is saying, "My father will *not* march his children before the court"; thus the verbs κλάῃ and ὀλοφύρηται refer to others, not to the defense speakers themselves.[8]

Demosthenes predicts an appeal to pity at 19.310:

ἀλλ' ὑπὲρ αὑτοῦ κλαήσει τοῦ τὰ τοιαῦτα πεπρεσβευκότος, καὶ τὰ παιδί᾽ ἴσως παράξει κἀναβιβᾶται

He will shed tears for himself, and he will probably produce his children and bring them up.

In his speech *Against Meidias*, Demosthenes not only omits the hedging ἴσως, but claims that the appeal to pity is the defendant's only recourse:

τί οὖν ὑπόλοιπον; ἐλεῆσαι νὴ Δία· παιδία γὰρ παραστήσεται καὶ κλαήσει καὶ τούτοις αὐτὸν ἐξαιτήσεται· τοῦτο γὰρ λοιπόν.

What other defense is left? Pity, you may say: he'll bring forward children and weep and ask you to let him off for their sake – that's what's left.

Demosthenes 21.99 (my translation)

---

[7] A counterexample to the principle of *la solidarité de la famille*, the principal subject of Glotz 1904. For a grandfather's good deeds performed prophylactically, see Andocides 1.141 and Jost 1936:36. Demosthenes 25.84, a prosecution speech, endorses the general principle of extending pity when a litigant's family was put on display.

[8] Konstan 2001:40–41 analyzes the adroit pivot this passage executes.

Similarly, at §186 Demosthenes simply *knows* that Meidias will parade his children and lament:

οἶδα τοίνυν ὅτι τὰ παιδί᾽ ἔχων ὀδυρεῖται, καὶ πολλοὺς λόγους καὶ ταπεινοὺς ἐρεῖ, δακρύων καὶ ὡς ἐλεινότατον ποιῶν ἑαυτόν.

Now, I know that he'll have his children here too, and he'll lament and make a long humble speech, weeping and making himself as pitiable as possible. (My translation)

Demosthenes himself could be said to have staged a pitiable parade through words alone by describing the effect a loss in court would have on his mother and sister if he does not defeat Aphobus (Demosthenes 28.19–22). It should be noted, however, that this entire speech is exceptionally vehement.

Any prosecutor will, obviously, hope to disarm all appeals to pity voiced – or staged – by the defense. Merely to predict that the defendant will make such an appeal is to suggest that the gesture is contemptible, simply by virtue of being a cliché. Characterizing the appeal in advance as "weeping," "wailing," and "lamentation" demeans it further. In passages in the preserved speeches, those who invoke the jury's pity do not, obviously enough, choose to describe themselves as so demeaned; it is, nevertheless, all but certain that some litigants did carry on just as those who mocked them said they did. Otherwise the passages I have presented so far would have seemed like pointless canards. Self-abjection was for the professionals a distinct *evitandum*.[9]

Our expressions "appeal to pity," "appeal for mercy," or even the traditional "appeal *ad misericordiam*," color our view. ἔλεος and related words are associated with acknowledgement of wrongdoing (this is implied by the words *Kyrie, eleêson* in the Mass), an abject posture, a presentation of oneself to the world as weak and utterly helpless. When we read 'beseech' as a translation of δεόμεθα, the English word steers us into overestimating the speaker's wretchedness. Consider some examples from E. S. Forster's Loeb translation of Isaeus (1927). At 2.47 the speaker ends his speech with this appeal to the jury:

---

[9] Johnstone 1999:118 makes an astute point about the few instances in which a prosecutor in a *dikê* uses the plea *ad misericordiam*: almost all the prosecutors were orphans arguing for their inheritance. Johnstone remarks several times on the asymmetry between prosecutors and defendants and criticizes the view of litigation as basically a competition for honor (see his chap. 4). What he misses is the difference among speakers in navigating this treacherous part of a court presentation.

ἀλλ' ἐπειδὴ τὸ πρᾶγμα εἰς ὑμᾶς ἀφῖκται καὶ ὑμεῖς κύριοι γεγόνατε, βοηθήσατε καὶ ἡμῖν καὶ ἐκείνῳ τῷ ἐν Ἅιδου ὄντι, καὶ μὴ περιίδητε – <u>πρὸς θεῶν καὶ δαιμόνων δέομαι ὑμῶν</u> – προπηλακισθέντα αὐτὸν ὑπὸ τούτων, ἀλλὰ μεμνημένοι τοῦ νόμου καὶ τοῦ ὅρκου ὃν ὀμωμόκατε καὶ τῶν εἰρημένων ὑπὲρ τοῦ πράγματος, τὰ δίκαια καὶ τὰ εὔορκα κατὰ τοὺς νόμους ψηφίσασθε.

> ... but since the matter has come before you for judgment and you
> have the sovereign right of decision, come to the aid both of us
> and of him who is in the other world, and do not allow Menecles,
> *by the gods and deities I beseech you*, to be insulted by my opponents,
> but mindful of the law and of the oath which you have sworn and of
> the arguments which have been used in support of my plea, pass in
> accordance with the laws the verdict which is just and in conformity
> with your oath.

Forster's English for the underlined phrase, "by the gods and deities I beseech you," seems justified by the invocation of the supernatural world. And when linguistic associations of our own language are, evidently, augmented by the mention of supplication, which for our culture is an extreme form of self-debasement, we can easily fall into the assumption that the speaker is groveling, metaphorically or even literally. Just moments before the passage already cited the speaker had used a string of words that would seem to prove his desperation (2.44, again in Forster's translation):

ἐγὼ οὖν δέομαι ὑμῶν πάντων, ὦ ἄνδρες, καὶ ἀντιβολῶ καὶ ἱκετεύω ἐλεῆσαί με καὶ ἀποψηφίσασθαι τοῦ μάρτυρος τουτουί.

> I beg you all therefore, gentleman, and beseech and entreat you to
> pity me and to acquit the witness here.

On the other hand, δεῖσθαι need not by itself carry much pathos. At 5.20 the speaker asks (δεόμεθα; Forster: "we beseech") jurors who were present at a certain occasion for their assistance in informing the other members of the panel. In contemporary English, "ask" or "request" would better render the speaker's tone (these are the verbs chosen by MacDowell for his 2004 translation of Demosthenes 27–38). It is true that the very rich families involved in the dispute have lost much of their wealth, and commentators (e.g. Wyse 1904:44) regard the speaker's argument as weak. But the man is, as Wyse says, "not a novice in litigation," and the tone of the *epilogos* is hardly diffident.

The affective quality of the phrase ἀντιβολῶ καὶ ἱκετεύω, which often appears together with δέομαι in requests to the jury,[10] is not quite as easy to assess. Their original reference is to ritual acts meant to appease supernatural beings, yet the emotional level of this form of entreaty need not indicate an agitated or distressed speaker. Consider these five examples from Isaeus (translations now from Michael Edwards' 2007 translation in the Texas series):

(1) 2.2: δέομαι δ᾽ ὑμῶν ἁπάντων καὶ ἀντιβολῶ καὶ ἱκετεύω μετ᾽ εὐνοίας ἀποδέχεσθαί μου τοὺς λόγους.

I beg and entreat and supplicate you all to receive my speech with goodwill.

(2) 2.44.1–3: ἐγὼ οὖν δέομαι ὑμῶν πάντων, ὦ ἄνδρες, καὶ ἀντιβολῶ καὶ ἱκετεύω ἐλεῆσαί με καὶ ἀποψηφίσασθαι τοῦ μάρτυρος τουτουί.

I therefore beg and entreat and supplicate you all, gentlemen, to pity me and acquit the witness here.

(3) 6.57.3–8: τοῦτο γὰρ ὑμῶν δέομαι καὶ ἱκετεύω σφόδρα μεμνῆσθαι, ὦ ἄνδρες, ὅπερ ὀλίγῳ πρότερον ἀπέδειξα ὑμῖν, ὅτι Ἀνδροκλῆς οὑτοσὶ φησὶ μὲν εἶναι ἐπίτροπος αὐτῶν ὡς ὄντων γνησίων Εὐκτήμονος, εἴληχε δ᾽ αὐτὸς ἑαυτῷ τοῦ Εὐκτήμονος κλήρου καὶ τῆς θυγατρὸς αὐτοῦ ὡς οὔσης ἐπικλήρου·

I beg and earnestly supplicate you to remember, gentlemen, what I described to you just now, that Androcles here says he's the guardian of our opponents whom he alleges are the legitimate sons of Euctemon, but he himself claimed for himself Euctemon's estate and his daughter as heiress.

(4) 8.45.1–4: ὑμῶν δ᾽ ἐγὼ δέομαι καὶ ἱκετεύω, μή με περιίδητε περὶ τούτων ὑβρισθέντα τῶν χρημάτων ὧν ὁ πάππος κατέλιπε, μηδ᾽ ἀποστερηθέντα, ἀλλὰ βοηθήσατε καθ᾽ ὅσον ὑμῶν ἕκαστος τυγχάνει δυνάμενος.

---

[10] In the proem of the same speech (2.2), for instance, appealing to the jury to listen with good will.

But I beg and supplicate you, do not allow me to be insulted and deprived of this estate that my grandfather left, but help me as far as each of you is able.

(5) fr. 4.1 Thalheim: δέομαι οὖν ὑμῶν συγγνώμην ἔχειν, εἰ καὶ νεώτερος ὢν λέγειν ἐπὶ δικαστηρίου τετόλμηκα· διὰ γὰρ τοὺς ἀδικοῦντας ἀναγκάζομαι παρὰ τὸν ἐμαυτοῦ τρόπον τοιοῦτόν τι ποιεῖν. πειράσομαι δ' ὑμῖν ἐξ ἀρχῆς ὡς ἂν δύνωμαι διὰ βραχυτάτων εἰπεῖν περὶ τοῦ πράγματος.

I beg you, therefore, to excuse me if, young as I still am, I have ventured to speak before a court.

The repeated collocation of the three verbs suggests a formula, almost a cliché – not that the use of a cliché must exclude emotion (Johnstone 1999:172n41).[11] Still, the near identity of the first two examples is, at the least, an indication that the speakers were following a template, and that the same words would be appropriate both to a preliminary *captatio benevolentiae* (in the first example) and to approach the speech's conclusion (in the second), a point where we would expect a warmer rhetorical temperature. In the third, the request involves a recollection of a specific fact. Against these examples we can hold another passage from Isaeus (8.22) that is undoubtedly meant to describe – not enact – powerful emotion at work:

δεομένης δὲ τῆς τοῦ πάππου γυναικὸς ἐκ τῆς οἰκίας αὐτὸν ἐκείνης θάπτειν καὶ λεγούσης ὅτι βούλοιτ' ἂν αὐτὴ τὸ σῶμα τὸ ἐκείνου συμμεταχειρίζεσθαι μεθ' ἡμῶν καὶ κοσμῆσαι, καὶ ταῦτα ἱκετευούσης καὶ κλαιούσης, ἐπείσθην, ὦ ἄνδρες, καὶ τούτῳ προσελθὼν μαρτύρων ἐναντίον εἶπον ὅτι ἐντεῦθεν ποιήσομαι τὴν ταφήν, δεδεημένη γὰρ εἴη ταῦτα ποιεῖν ἡ τούτου ἀδελφή.

But when my grandfather's widow asked me to bury him from that house, and with supplications and tears said that she herself would like to help us lay out and adorn his body, I consented, gentlemen. I went to our opponent and told him in front of witnesses that I would conduct the funeral from there because Diocles' sister had begged me to do so.

---

[11] For doubling of synonyms to add emphasis, especially with the verb δέομαι, see Slings and de Stryker ad Plato *Apology* 171c6.

Here we have not a first-person address but a narrative; the subject is a mature, possibly old woman; the occasion is her husband's funeral; moreover, she is reported to have wept. The occasion and the agent are compatible with an emotional outburst. This seems to me utterly distinct from the nearly formulaic requests with which it shares some vocabulary. When an expert speaker like the ex-actor Aeschines presented his aged father and, perhaps, mother at 2.147–148,[12] he had the means to excite pity by vocal inflections and posture, whether drawn from life or from stage conventions. By virtue of his age alone, the spectacle of his ninety-four-year-old father was no doubt capable of exciting pity. But the entire passage, which runs from 146–152, is filled with objective claims about his family's rectitude and public services, a list that seems ill suited to histrionic delivery.[13]

In a general article aiming to give an account "both of the institution [of supplication] and of its place and significance in the fabric of Greek social institutions," John Gould argued that what he terms "figurative supplication" was veering to the "more or less empty metaphorical." And he regards the appeals to pity directed to juries as the "paradigm case" of figurative supplication (Gould 1973:78n24, 101). Johnstone acknowledges that "litigants sometimes used the language of supplication in attenuated and metaphorical ways, as when a litigant 'supplicates' a jury to listen in silence or simply hear his case." But he continues, "Nevertheless, though formalized, the language of supplication was itself powerful and was linked, furthermore, to socially meaningful practices," adducing the frequent supplication scenes in tragedy. For Johnstone, the power and meaning adhering to supplication as a ritual, even in a much reduced form, is to be understood as a "cognitive, not emotional, social event," and for that reason he insists that "the contemporary

---

[12] We cannot tell whether Aeschines' words about her, prefaced by ἢ νῦν ἐμοὶ πρὸ τῶν ὀφθαλμῶν προφαίνεται, mean that she was alive and present in court or vivid in Aeschines' imagination: see Fisher 2001 ad loc. and 16.

[13] The speaker of Lysias 24, who defends his eligibility for the one-obol welfare payment (on the matter of authenticity see chapter 2), makes no claim of significant services to the state, only that during the civil war he left the city together with other democrats (25). His appeal at §§7–8 has a piteous ring ("Do not utterly destroy me. . . . Do not have the hard-heartedness to wrong me, and so cause others in my position to despair"); yet the tone so quickly turns jokey that the speaker's recovery, as it were, might be intended to suggest that the logographos was eager to have his client show himself capable of self-possession.

institution of Athenian tragic theater provides no basis for understanding pity in the courts" (Johnstone 1999:116 with n44, 121)[14]

Though I agree that the cognitive element of appeals to pity is significant (see below on Konstan's interpretation), it is going too far to exclude emotion as exerting a force that we can, with some probability, ascertain. I grant that the interplay between cognition and emotion is complex, and that group dynamics can on occasion supersede the individual, perhaps by the manipulation of *thorubos* (Bers 1985; Lanni 1997). Johnstone's argument that we cannot speak of the emotions of a collective body such as a jury or a theater audience strikes me (if I understand it right) as a great exaggeration, at odds not only with our intuition that in a properly run trial the jurors react as individuals and maintain a high, if not total, degree of independent judgment. Consequently, there is value in assessing the affect expressed in pleas for pity. The physical gestures of paradigmatic supplication, a certain physical pose and physical contact, are virtually absent or replaced by the manipulation of a physical object not directly connected to the speech.[15] This does not seem to me a convincing argument, but not because of the treatment of those physical features. Rather, the tone suggested by the relevant passages in professional speech seems to me *untheatrical*; hence I cannot accept the affinity to stage drama that Johnstone proposes (Johnstone 1999:116 with n44). The skilled court speaker might well be working to arouse strong affect in the jury, but he

[14] Johnstone points out (1999:172n43) that Demosthenes never "supplicates" the Ecclesia, perhaps because "this reflects a different relationship between speakers and audience in the Assembly, and in the courts." Perhaps, though the language of supplication, even when used in an attenuated form in asking for the jury's sympathy, was felt to be inappropriate when applied to deliberations over policy. A further wrinkle: Johnstone argues several pages later (1999:120–122) that in Athenian culture pity must be understood primarily in terms of cognition, and he insists that "the contemporary institution of Athenian tragic theater provides no basis for understanding pity in the courts." I agree with Johnstone's conclusion that litigants are presenting "cognitive claims," but not the adjective he attaches to that phrase, "implicit."

[15] Johnstone 1999:116–117 thoroughly mines the evidence for physical acts that might count as supplication, but I see no reason to doubt that a speaker's verbal appeal for pity involved nothing of the kind. At 175n70 he adduces Demosthenes 58.8.70, but that is the speaker's description of supplication he performed at an earlier trial ("I supplicated him at his knees"). Moreover, the speaker probably never spoke at that earlier trial (he describes himself as young: §§1–3); and the speech as a whole has struck scholars as the product of a "second-rate" writer (*inter alios* Schaeffer 1858:3.279–80). At 169n4 Johnstone mentions the argument put forth by Navarre that in Greek oratory appeals to pity were acted out, but in ways that the texts do not record (cf. Kennedy 1991:154n76 ad Aristotle *Rhetoric* 1386a: "defendants in Greek courts probably sometimes dressed for the part to awaken sympathy"). *If* this was an actual practice, it would, in my opinion, be the desperate expedient of an amateur litigant. An argument from silence, of course, but perhaps true as applied to speeches at an amateur level far distant from the activities of the professional *logographoi*.

himself does not seem to me to be adopting a style that implicitly or explicitly suggests that he is in the grip of emotion.

Aristotle's remarks on rhetorical delivery in the *Rhetoric*, e.g. at 1386a30–b7, which, like much of that work, make frequent jumps to theatrical practice, are more frustrating than helpful. It would be enormously helpful to know just how broad or restrained, how stylized or natural, were the "gestures and cries, and displays of feelings, and generally [the] acting" (trans. Kennedy 1991) to which he alludes. Aristotle seems tripped up by his disdain for the inescapable role played by *hypokrisis* in forensic and political speech, and I see nothing in the *Rhetoric* that leads to any useful comparison between a court speaker and an actor making something "vivid." The more flamboyant style of speaking prominent in Aristotle's own time, especially in Demosthenes and Aeschines, further muddies the waters. The best treatment I have seen is Sifakis 2002, but I confess to a persistent feeling of frustration.

At the close of his defense against Demosthenes' charges that he had become Philip's tool, Aeschines presents to the jury a large entourage of relatives. The passage holds within itself an indication of how it was delivered:

κἀμοὶ μὲν οἱ συνδεησόμενοι πάρεισιν ὑμῶν πατὴρ μέν, οὗ τὰς τοῦ γήρως ἐλπίδας μὴ ἀφέλησθε, ἀδελφοὶ δέ, οἳ διαζυγέντες ἐμοῦ ζῆν οὐκ ἂν προέλοιντο, κηδεσταὶ δὲ καὶ ταυτὶ τὰ μικρὰ μὲν παιδία καὶ τοὺς κινδύνους οὔπω συνιέντα, ἐλεεινὰ δ' εἴ τι συμβήσεται παθεῖν ἡμῖν. ὑπὲρ ὧν ἐγὼ δέομαι καὶ ἱκετεύω πολλὴν πρόνοιαν ποιήσασθαι, καὶ μὴ τοῖς ἐχθροῖς αὐτοὺς μηδ' ἀνάνδρῳ καὶ γυναικείῳ τὴν ὀργὴν ἀνθρώπῳ παραδοῦναι.

There are people here to join me in imploring you: my father – do not deprive him of his hopes for his old age; my brothers, who would not want to live if I were taken from them; my in-laws; and these little children who do not yet recognize the danger but who will be pitiful if anything befalls me. I beg and implore you to give careful thought to them and not hand them over to their enemies or to this person of unmanly and effeminate temperament.

Aeschines 2.179 (trans. Carey 2000, but with
the final phrase more literally rendered)

In the last sentence Aeschines condemns Demosthenes as "unmanly and effeminate in his temperament [*orgê*]," which is implicitly contrasted with his own and his family's masculinity. Aeschines is, to be sure, asking the jurors, and even the gods, to save him from execution (see §180; cf. Demosthenes 19.31), but the contrast he implies between Demosthenes and himself indicates (if it does not prove) that he was guarding against any sign that he was exhibiting the very weakness he hoped to pin on his enemy.

For economy of presentation, I proceed to brief remarks on the speaker's self-characterization in a few of the passages cited by Konstan (2001:43) to demonstrate the thesis of his first chapter. His claim, which I find entirely persuasive, is that "pity, in the classical conception ... was not something separate and apart from judgments concerning justice and desert, but rather presupposed the innocence ... of the accused party. For this reason, an appeal to pity was not accompanied by expressions of remorse, nor a request for pardon or forgiveness; it was designed rather to make vivid to the jury the consequences of condemning an innocent person." Seen this way, the fundamental intent of these appeals as they are composed by professionals is compatible with a dignified delivery.

On Lysias 21.24–25, Konstan (2001:38) remarks:

> The speaker's intention is to contrast as sharply as possible what his character and history of service to the state ought to earn him with the harsh consequences of a negative verdict. He is not for a moment suggesting that he be spared on the basis of his good deeds or character, *in spite of* the wrongs he may have committed while holding public office. Rather, he is making vivid to the jury what losing his case would mean for himself and his family, precisely on the assumption that he is innocent. His object is not to ask for mercy, in the sense in which mercy presupposes guilt ... ; it is to make sure that no irrelevant motive, such as personal hostility, political partisanship, or favour toward his accuser, may induce the jury to convict him, by making clear what is at stake if they do so. It is a way of charging the jury to take seriously the power at their disposal, and be certain that they do not do grave harm, as they can, on the basis of insufficient evidence, when the charges involving bribery are all the more implausible in light of his history of selfless service to the city.

To this we can add that at §§4 and 24 the speaker claims to have been stoic under circumstances of physical danger.

The speaker at Lysias 7.41 presents a catalog of the misery he will face if convicted:

πάντων γὰρ ἀθλιώτατος ἂν γενοίμην, εἰ φυγὰς ἀδίκως κατα-
στήσομαι, ἄπαις μὲν ὢν καὶ μόνος, ἐρήμου δὲ τοῦ οἴκου γενομένου,
μητρὸς δὲ πάντων ἐνδεοῦς <οὔσης>, πατρίδος δὲ τοιαύτης ἐπ'
αἰσχίσταις στερηθεὶς αἰτίαις, πολλὰς μὲν ναυμαχίας ὑπὲρ αὐτῆς
νεναυμαχηκώς, πολλὰς δὲ μάχας μεμαχημένος, κόσμιον δ' ἐμαυτὸν
καὶ ἐν δημοκρατίᾳ καὶ ἐν ὀλιγαρχίᾳ παρασχών.

I would be the most wretched of all men, if I were unjustly forced
into exile. I would be childless and alone. My household would be
made desolate. My mother would be stripped of everything. I would
be deprived, on charges that bring extreme pain, of the native land
which means so much to me, for which I have fought many battles
on land and at sea, and have behaved well under both democracy
and oligarchy.

Despite projecting the picture of his future life as superlatively wretched
(ἀθλιώτατος), the defendant cites his military, which is to say his manly,
achievements. In the second clause of the last sentence he boasts that he has
been consistently *kosmios*, the very quality I have proposed as encapsulating
the "civic personality" skillful forensic speech aimed to display.[16] Manliness
did not exclude manifestations of happiness and grief in private,[17] but in court
a man was well advised to keep a stiff upper lip even when – perhaps especially
when – he was asking for pity.

Displaying Anger

Anger is another emotion that has attracted much scholarly attention since
the late 1990s (e.g. Allen 2000, Braund and Most 2003), and it is certainly
present in the verbal surface of many forensic and political speeches. Athenian
attitudes to anger were ambivalent (see W. Harris 2001, chap. 8, esp. 183–187),

---

[16] I summarize here the most relevant points in a couple of other examples, ostensibly appeals
for pity, treated by Konstan 2001, adding some remarks of my own. On Lysias 4.20 Konstan
(2001:39) writes: "The appeal to pity is not a means of distracting the jurors from the evidence
relevant to the case, but rather of enjoining them to judge in accordance with the facts and
with justice, and not heedlessly impose a penalty that will cause an innocent man to suffer
gravely, and thus in truth be pitiable." Note that at 7.41 the speaker claims to have been stoic
(*kosmios*) in battles on land and sea. Not surprisingly, prosecutors might be said to share the
defendants' contention that guilty men deserve no pity (Konstan 2001:41, citing *inter alia*
Lysias 14.40).

[17] See Roisman 2005:54, commenting on Apollodorus' self-reported emotions in [Demosthenes] 53.

but the lawcourt context certainly favors assertions of the social value of self-restraint in the face of nearly unbearable provocation (see my discussion of *egkrateia* in chapter 5). And as with pity, the other emotion that Thrasymachus is said to have taught men to manipulate (see the first section of this chapter), the text is not a reliable indication of the speaker's actual, unsimulated affect and the degree to which a skilled rhetorical performance would manifest any particular emotion. An orator may *say* he is angry, but that does not in itself entail a visible loss of *egkrateia* (self-possession), much less that his blood is really at full boil when he strives to arouse anger in his audience.[18]

At the start and conclusion of the *Rhetoric* (1354a17; 1419b26), and many times in between, Aristotle speaks of orators' need to arouse ὀργή, anger, in their audiences, but anger is, for him, one of those regrettable phenomena of oratory that would have no place in a well-ordered society because it is πρὸς δικαστήν ("directed to the juryman" [1354a18]). That cranky formulation seems to ignore anger in the speaker, but elsewhere in the *Rhetoric* Aristotle does recognize that a speaker's style (*lexis*) can exhibit too chill a sangfroid and thereby endanger his credibility:

παθητικὴ δέ, ἐὰν μὲν ᾖ ὕβρις, ὀργιζομένου λέξις, ἐὰν δὲ ἀσεβῆ καὶ αἰσχρά, δυσχεραίνοντος καὶ εὐλαβουμένου καὶ λέγειν, ἐὰν δὲ ἐπαινετά, ἀγαμένως, ἐὰν δὲ ἐλεεινά, ταπεινῶς, καὶ ἐπὶ τῶν ἄλλων δὲ ὁμοίως. πιθανοῖ δὲ τὸ πρᾶγμα καὶ ἡ οἰκεία λέξις· παραλογίζεταί τε γὰρ ἡ ψυχὴ ὡς ἀληθῶς λέγοντος, ὅτι ἐπὶ τοῖς τοιούτοις οὕτως ἔχουσιν, ὥστ' οἴονται, εἰ καὶ μὴ οὕτως ἔχει ὡς λέγει ὁ λέγων, τὰ πράγματα οὕτως ἔχειν, καὶ συνομοπαθεῖ ὁ ἀκούων ἀεὶ τῷ παθητικῶς λέγοντι, κἂν μηθὲν λέγῃ. διὸ πολλοὶ καταπλήττουσι τοὺς ἀκροατὰς θορυβοῦντες.

Emotion is expressed if the style, in the case of insolence [*hybris*], is that of an angry man; in the case of impious and shameful things, if it is that of one who is indignant and reluctant even to say the words; in the case of admirable things, [if they are spoken] respectfully; but if [the things] are pitiable, [if they are spoken] in a submissive manner; and similarly in other cases. The proper *lexis* also makes the matter credible: the mind [of the listener] draws a false

---

[18] A further complication: the word ὀργή might have a connotation in lawcourt speech rather different from the apparent plain meaning. MacDowell comments on Demosthenes 19.91: "as often in forensic speeches, this word refers not primarily to the emotion of anger but to conviction in court." A controversial reading of the word, but not one that can be easily dismissed.

inference of the truth what a speaker says because they [in the audience] feel the same about such things, so they think the facts to be so, even if they are not as the speaker represents them; and the hearer suffers along with the pathetic speaker, even if what he says amounts to nothing As a result, many overwhelm their hearers by making noise.

Rhetoric 1408a16–25 (trans. Kennedy 1991 –
but see the discussion immediately following)

At first reading, this may seem to recommend a frankly mimetic style, advice that would of course threaten my general thesis – that professional speech aimed at the restraint of speakers' affect – but Aristotle is not going that far. The interpretation of the last sentence is crucial, for it appears to report that a plangent delivery succeeds in Attic courts; worse, a style both plangent and dishonest. The speakers who are so characterized may well be working to overcome an objective deficiency in the honesty of their pleadings.[19] And in the next section Aristotle appears to recommend naturalism in forensic speech:

οὐ γὰρ ταὐτὰ οὐδ᾽ ὡσαύτως ἀγροῖκος ἂν καὶ πεπαιδευμένος εἴπειεν.

A rustic and an educated person would not say the same thing nor [say it] in the same way.

Rhetoric 1408a31–32 (trans. Kennedy 1991)

It is important to keep in mind that Aristotle is habitually aware of gradations, even if he does not make the point explicitly at every step, and there is no reason to think that his prescriptions here are deviations from his ingrained practice. Very soon he is back to his usual caution:

τὸ δ᾽ εὐκαίρως ἢ μὴ εὐκαίρως χρῆσθαι κοινὸν ἁπάντων τῶν εἰδῶν ἐστιν.

---

[19] Aristotle is optimistic at *Rhetoric* 1355a22, claiming that the truth is by its nature more powerful than the false: χρήσιμος δέ ἐστιν ἡ ῥητορικὴ διά τε τὸ φύσει εἶναι κρείττω τἀληθῆ καὶ τὰ δί.καια τῶν ἐναντίων, ὥστε ἐὰν μὴ κατὰ τὸ προσῆκον αἱ κρίσεις γίγνωνται, ἀνάγκη δι᾽ αὐτῶν ἡττᾶσθαι. . . .

Opportune or inopportune usage is a factor common to all [three] species of rhetoric.

Rhetoric 1408b1–2 (trans. Kennedy 1991)

And his specific advice requires a deliberate calibration and recalibration of the artful and the ingenuous:

ἔτι τοῖς ἀνάλογον μὴ πᾶσιν ἅμα χρήσασθαι (οὕτω γὰρ κλέπτεται ὁ ἀκροατής)· λέγω δὲ οἷον ἐὰν τὰ ὀνόματα σκληρὰ ᾖ, μὴ καὶ τῇ φωνῇ καὶ τῷ προσώπῳ τοῖς ἁρμόττουσιν· εἰ δὲ μή, φανερὸν γίνεται ἕκαστον ὅ ἐστιν. ἐὰν δὲ τὸ μὲν τὸ δὲ μή, λανθάνει ποιῶν τὸ αὐτό. ἐὰν οὖν τὰ μαλακὰ σκληρῶς καὶ τὰ σκληρὰ μαλακῶς λέγηται, πιθανὸν γίγνεται.

[D]o not use all analogous effects [of sounds and sense] together; for thus the hearer is tricked. I mean, for example, if the words are harsh, do not deliver them with a harsh voice and countenance. Otherwise, what you are doing is evident. But if sometimes one feature is present, sometimes not, you accomplish the same thing without being noticed. But if, as a result, gentle things are said harshly and harsh things gently, the result is unpersuasive.

Rhetoric 1408b4–10 (trans. Kennedy 1991)

Note the sequence. The text has moved from (a) a suggestion that shouting in the disorderly manner of crowds (θορυβοῦντες) might be effective, to (b) the advice to make the delivery run counter to the words' meanings, to (c) a warning not to allow the mismatch of surface content and delivery to go too far. Aristotle is not, after all, suggesting that one go to court and "let it all hang out."[20] There is a tantalizing generic mention of professional speechwriters at 1404a34 (one of just three appearances in the *Rhetoric* of the word *logographos*), but no explicit comment on how they would usually advise a client on the matter of emotionalism in the composition and delivery of a speech. It would be particularly interesting to know how a professional would advice the rustic (ἀγροῖκος), whose style Aristotle says would be different from that of an educated man (πεπαιδευμένος).

---

[20] Consequently I prefer the Rhys Roberts translation of 1408a23–25, even though it stretches the conative element of the imperfective present: "an emotional speaker always makes his audience feel with him, even when there is nothing in his arguments; which is why many speakers *try to overwhelm* their audience by mere noise."

Perhaps Cicero was on to something when he reports – or possibly boasts – that he used an extensive repertory to make jurymen angry, that he himself felt anger,[21] and that in this respect his only predecessor was Demosthenes. One reading of Aristophanes' *Wasps* can imprint the insect's fury on our imagination, but Philocleon and his swarm come on stage as the targeted audience of forensic display, not as skilled practitioners of the art.

Prima facie, a court speaker's displays of anger might seem less vulnerable to suspicions of unmanliness, or might even win a favorable reaction from jurymen. Anger is, after all, an emotion that buttresses martial valor; it can, far more pertinently, manifest the proper stance toward classes of persons who injure society. (Aristotle introduces a relevant terminological distinction at *Rhetoric* 1382a1–7, calling *orgê* an emotion aimed merely at individuals, *misos* the emotion aimed against thieves and sycophants.)[22] On the other hand, control of anger is a notably pervasive and conspicuous theme in literature and philosophy throughout the ancient world, and the urgency of restraining and channeling anger is nowhere seen in a greater variety of ways than in our evidence for Athens in the fifth and fourth centuries. It will be sufficient here to refer to the eighth chapter of W. Harris 2001. And just as I do not regard explicit appeals to pity in professional oratory as proof that the speaker was to enact his piteousness, I do not interpret a speaker's report of his own anger as reliable evidence that he was to manifest rage as he spoke. Here it is crucial to analyze the tone of the Greek as precisely as we can. To my eyes, it is misleading to punctuate with exclamation marks as Allen (2003:76) has done in translating Demosthenes *Against Meidias* 21.123: "All this bad behavior and his habit of adding to the troubles of people who justly defend themselves against him must be paid back with more than just my getting angry and upset while you look the other way! It's necessary for everyone to be just as angry!" Moreover, the dramatizing inceptive force of "getting angry" is far from certain in the verb ἀγανακτεῖν, and βαρέως φέρειν does not seem to me to suggest that Demosthenes reports himself as "all shook up" (cf. MacDowell's translation of both parts as "resent indignantly"). Similarly, I do not accept Allen's assertion (2003:81) that "[t]he expectation that orators should prove their hot blood, as it were, is also clear from the regularity with which orators display discomfort about delayed prosecutions."

Rubinstein's investigation of dicastic anger indicates the risks in attempting to manipulate the jury's anger, particularly in private cases.

---

[21] *Orator* 131–133. See W. Harris 2001:111 with n124.
[22] This is clearly explained in Rubinstein 2004:193 with n18.

Rubinstein remarks (2004:190) that "whatever self-regulation [of the arguments litigants presented] there may have been in Athens would have been exercised by the individual litigants – or their logographers – who would have been constrained only by tactical considerations, not by any consideration of general ethical principles. The crucial tactical decisions made by the author of a forensic speech would have to be made on the basis of what he assumed would be acceptable to the audience." To this we can add that an individual amateur litigant, lacking the logographer's restraining hand, would more likely yield to his emotions and allow his rage to break out, thereby offending his judges and harming his case.

7

TACTICS, AMATEUR AND PROFESSIONAL

I N REMARKING ON THE STYLE OF CLASSICAL GREEK AUTHORS, moderns usually leave denigration to the ancients.[1] Criticisms such as MacDowell's remarks on Andocides' stylistic lapses (1962:20–22) are exceptional.[2] And there is an obvious reason for us to be slow to censure: we have very little poorly written literature from the fifth and fourth centuries. In their choice of diction in the strict sense of lexicon, we rarely have grounds to suspect authors of confusions of register. No poet could compose without a mastery of prosody, and Attic prose writers were soon mindful, at least to some degree, of rhythm. We can infer that this is very largely a matter of conscious procedure from the fact that all these aspects of writing receive explicit attention in surviving texts, starting with Gorgias' remarks on diction in the *Encomium of Helen* (55). But it should go without saying that no one should draw lines of demarcation between conscious and unconscious stylistic choice with any great confidence. Surviving ancient sources tell us nothing about some phenomena discovered by moderns, such as "Porson's bridge" and many other prosodic restrictions in verse; but there are texts that show that a skilled Greek author did not need to wait for Denniston to be aware of another author's individual preference: Plato almost certainly noticed Lysias' love of καὶ μὲν δή and saw its value in his mock-Lysianic (or so I am convinced) *Erotikos* in the *Phaedrus* (Dimock 1952:392, with references to earlier work; Denniston 1954: lxxx). This brings me to the subject of the next few pages, the use of particles.

---

[1] One thinks of Pratinas fr. 3 Snell on his competitors' noise, Aeschylus deriding Euripides and vice versa in the *Frogs*, Aristotle *Rhetoric* 1504a on inept use of poetic vocabulary, Plutarch *Moralia* 350e on Isocrates' dread of hiatus, Dionysius of Halicarnassus *On Thucydides* 21–49.

[2] "Andokides sometimes tries to impose antithetical form on his matter and fails. . . . [He] gets the contrasts muddled. . . . Lysianic simplicity is hard to achieve, and Andokides often fails to achieve it. . . . He often interrupts the flow of a sentence by inserting a clumsy parenthesis, or even breaks off altogether and begins a fresh sentence without ever completing the construction of the previous one."

Particles

The particles hold a special benefit for the stylistic analysis of Greek authors as the "small change" of language (I owe the expression to Benedict Einarson), a medley of nearly all short words with little or no lexical meaning per se, and hence the sort of detail that a professional writer is far more likely to notice than a layman.

In his Sather lectures, K. J. Dover (1968b:83) demonstrates that "in the Lysian period a certain distance between forensic language and colloquial language was maintained."[3] Specifically, "the outstanding difference between comic and forensic narrative is that ἔπειτα, ἔπειτα δέ, κἄπειτα, εἶτα, and κᾆτα [to introduce successive events, rather than as logical connectives] occur 23 times in Aristophanes," whereas "in forensic oratory these words are the rarest of all simple connectives"; moreover, a counterexample at Lysias 1.14 occurs within a short stretch of speech reported in *oratio recta* (Dover 1968b:84–85; cf. Bers 1997:183). Conversely, the orators in Dover's sample quite often use a sentence-initial participle or subordinate clause followed by δέ in narration, whereas there is only one such example in comic narrative. "In this respect, even the plainest-seeming forensic narrative is close to historiography and far distant from the lively narrative of comedy" (Dover 1968b:85–86). (A demurral I must not omit: for the reasons I present in chapter 2 and in this chapter, I am in this monograph arguing that the "plainest-seeming narrative" available for our inspection is by no means the plainest narrative pronounced before an Athenian court.) Dover returned to these signals of temporal sequence in *The Evolution of Greek Prose Style* (1997:73–77), broadening his survey to include early prose narrative (Pherecydes and Acusilaus) and historiography (Herodotus, Thucydides, Xenophon). He concludes (1997:77), "It thus appears that a phenomenon shared by rehearsed and unrehearsed oral narrative and so portrayed in comedy affected the earliest written historical narrative but was used very sparingly by historians from Herodotus onward and by orators." I would reject the term "unrehearsed," which must refer to the quoted "live speech" in Lysias,[4] but the evidence en masse does quite certainly point to a linguistic feature relevant

---

[3] Dover does not here let us into his workshop, but presumably he does not reject Fraenkel's characterization of the connectives found in narratives in comedy (see Dover 1968b:83n33, a reference to Fraenkel 1962:126–127) as "primitive." An autobiographical irrelevance: more than anything else, Dover's analysis gave me the initial shove that has culminated in this monograph.

[4] This is not to say that every *logographos* would be as skilled as Lysias in reproducing or simulating a subtle feature of everyday speech with the intent of giving his client a mark of authenticity in reporting speech.

to forensic speech performed without professional assistance. It seems highly probable that amateurs required to speak in court would spend proportionally more of their time on the *bêma* simply telling the jury what they claimed had happened than those speakers who could afford the help of a man like Lysias, and would automatically use the same linguistic means to demarcate stages in the narrative that they used in routine speech. As Dover points out, the logographers place a subordinate clause or participle at the head of sentences and introduce the next event with a connective δέ; not so characters who recite long narratives in Aristophanes in a diction assumed to reflect colloquial speech. In this particular matter of narrative connectives a comparison to English usage might be useful. A chain of "and then"s is characteristic of children's speech; only with increasing age and sophistication do the tellers of narrative begin to emphasize instead the logical connections they see among events and use other devices to link the stages in their story. For logographers, the value of having the story under control, as it were, had the important advantage of suggesting that the speaker himself was under control. A ride on the shoulders of Denniston's *Greek Particles* reveals a large number of similar trends and a number of strictly observed rules. I have looked especially for affective qualities and patterns that help locate professional forensic speech in relation to "formal prose" on the one hand and colloquial speech on the other.[5] I discuss first some particle usages largely or entirely avoided in the surviving speeches. Not all examples in this category are truly germane, though for a variety of reasons. Some particles were excluded from oratory for reasons of dialect. For instance, what Denniston calls "ancillary" uses of οὖν in the combinations εἴτ' οὖν and οὔτ' οὖν in tragedy, Herodotus, and Plato (that is, what he terms the "semi-Ionic group") never appear in oratory or comedy (lxxi). Similarly, connective καὶ δή (lxxi–lxxii). This being a usage in the semi-Ionic group, it is not relevant to the present study. Or in some cases the distributional facts are irrelevant to the professional/amateur distinctions I am tracking, as in the case of ἦ. The particle is "affirmative, mostly with adjectives and adverbs. This is mainly a verse idiom, and is hardly found at all in oratory, except for ἦ μήν . . . , and the common use of ἦ που in *a fortiori* argument" (280). For the latter, Denniston gives only a single comic example (Aristophanes *Thesmophoriazusae* 63), which suggests either that the usage was not colloquial or, more likely, that it was too intellectual for most comic repartee. Similarly, ταῦτ' ἄρα, a particle combination never found in oratory. Denniston (37) translates it "I see: that's why. . . ." This might have been a common feature of colloquial Attic: I find 14 examples in Aristophanes (none of them in the

---

[5] In what follows, quotations in English and parenthetical page references are to Denniston 1954.

two fourth-century plays). Discovery of some truth in the course of speech is likely only if a man was (or could pretend to be) startled by something an opponent said in *his* speech, and the published version of the text reproduced an ex tempore modification of what the speaker had intended to say.

ἄρα "express[es] a lively feeling of interest. . . . Its character is quite foreign to the more formal style of Thucydides and the orators" (33). Denniston shows only two examples of this specific usage in orators. The phrasing in both is worth a look. At Antiphon 6.35 ἄρα punctuates an interjection: αὐτοῖς ἐκ μὲν τῶν πεπραγμένων οὐδεμία ἦν ἐλπὶς ἀποφεύξεσθαι – τοιαῦτα ἄρ' ἦν τὰ ἠδικημένα – ("Considering what they had done – so serious were their crimes – " [my translation]).

At Lysias 3.29–30 we find something similar: . . . ἔτυπτέ με. καὶ τότε μὲν ἄρα, ἵνα μὴ περιβόητος εἴην, ἡσυχίαν ἦγον, συμφορὰν ἐμαυτοῦ νομίζων τὴν τούτου πονηρίαν. A free translation, aiming to give full weight to the particle, might run ". . . he attacked me. And at *that* point in my life – get this!⁶ – I kept quiet." There are enough examples in Aristophanes (35) that I feel confident that the usage found its way from time to time into appropriate spots of narrative in amateur speech.

Despite the impression that Plato's *Apology* is likely to make on elementary students, interrogation of opponents is extremely rare in the speeches, at least to the degree that our texts display it (see Carawan 1983). My intuition is that *idiôtai* would from time to time be unable to restrain themselves from asking the other side questions they thought quite devastating.⁷ For that reason the distribution of δαί might be relevant. Denniston comments: "That it is a colloquial particle is clear from its frequency in Aristophanes and its complete absence from formal prose" (262). Opportunities for its use in oratory abound, as they do in Attic comedy and tragedy, both in rhetorical questions per se and in transitions (though not as "connective, in a question motivated by what precedes" [263], since that would suggest a two-voice dialogue, which is almost never found in oratory). Perhaps its function in questions was filled instead by the fundamentally redundant διὰ τί (roughly, "on account of – why?"), which is quite common in oratory starting with Antiphon (6.45); but it must be acknowledged that δαί might have become very scarce and then disappeared altogether in the fourth century, especially if we

---

⁶ Carey ad loc. cites Denniston 38–39, but the category there presented is "in reported speech, and after verbs of thinking and seeming," and of the many rhetorical examples Denniston lists, only one (Demosthenes 19.160) has the particle unsupported by ὡς.

⁷ Thereby violating the lawyers' maxim: never ask a witness a question to which you do not know the answer.

exclude the possible examples in Plato, a writer who used many fifth-century expressions.[8] But I believe a flavor of disconcerted, almost histrionic exasperation clung, though subtly, to the word δαί, making it an *evitandum*.

The analysis of δῆτα, which occurs nearly 95 times in Aristophanes, also involves questions and answers. The particle is "not common in the orators, but frequent in Plato, and exceedingly frequent in drama. There are only 9 examples in Demosthenes . . ." (269). I find a total of 19 examples in the TLG orators, all with οὐ or μή. The scarcity of this particle in orators is most probably an epiphenomenon of its affinity for questions and answers ("δῆτα is a lively particle, far more at home in question and answer than elsewhere" [269]). Plato uses the word twice in the *Apology* in the course of the interrogation of Meletus (284d), once with οὐ, once after τί. We might conclude that δῆτα is unlikely to have been heard in amateur court speech, but the frequency with which it appears in Aristophanes and the possibility that amateurs questioned their opponents more often than professionals cloud the issue.

In the use of που conveying the meaning "I think," a pervasive professional/amateur discrepancy is unlikely. Denniston (491) addresses the matter of "diffident" που directly:

> The tone of uncertainty, whether real or assumed, is ill-adapted to the precision of history, or to the assertiveness of oratory. There are . . . (in contrast with the free use of δήπου)[9] very few in the orators: Ant[iphon] v 6: Lys[ias] vi 25: Isoc[rates] xv 75: D[emosthenes] xxiii 162 (text doubtful). In D[emosthenes] xviii 51 που is perhaps local, . . . "somewhere in his speech": cf. xviii 299, πόρρω που "somewhere far."

An exceptionally diffident amateur litigant might have made the mistake of hedging with που (even one occurrence might have been too many), but it seems likely that in this detail at least most *idiôtai* and professionals would have followed the same practice.

About some other particles I have no hesitation in declaring the existence of a distinction between professional and amateur very probable. Two instances involve usages Denniston regards as bringing the speaker too close, metaphorically, to his audience. The orators, he says, "write works to be spoken to an audience, but there is no close personal touch between the speaker and

---

[8] Most prominently ἦν δ' ἐγώ and ἦ δ' ὅς for "I said" and "he said."
[9] One of the Demosthenic favorites (Denniston 1954:267–268); others are discussed later in the chapter.

the persons addressed."[10] Hence one is not surprised to find that "intimate particles like τοι or hortative ἀλλά are rare in oratory" (lxxiv; 14: hortatory ἀλλά "probably too intimate in tone"). These particles, especially τοι, are very likely to have been heard very often in amateur forensic speech: there are over 100 instances in Aristophanes. τοι's appearances in Antiphon did, quite naturally, puzzle Denniston: "[T]hat this most unbending and austere of orators should adopt towards the jury the kind of attitude that τοι implies, seems somehow not to fit" (lxxx). If it is not simply an inadvertence, Antiphon's ostensibly strange choice might explained as an experiment: see the discussion of the dramatic devices in his speech *Against the Stepmother* in chapter 3 above.

τοι seems to have gained some degree of further admittance into professional oratory by losing some of its warmth and immediacy in certain combinations. Schmidt 1891:41–43 observed that Demosthenes uses the particle only in conjunction with καὶ γάρ and ἐπεί. In the first of these (for distribution and citations see Denniston 113) a logical force is predominant, and the two occurrences in the Lysianic *Funeral Oration* indicate a controlled and solemn tone appropriate to the occasion. Denniston (553) finds ἤτοι only in Andocides 2.2, Isocrates 15.33, Demosthenes 14.40, 22.32, 25.51, 58.7, Aeschines 3.40, and Dinarchus 1.50; he adds that it does not occur in Antiphon (though he uses simple τοι relatively often), Isaeus, Lycurgus, or Hyperides.[11] I suggest that the rarity of the particle might reflect some persistence in the professionals' avoidance of τοι on its own, but there seems to be no reason to predict that the combinations would crop up with any frequency in amateur speech (there are no examples in Aristophanes).

About ἀτάρ Denniston (51) remarks:

> In prose, ἀτάρ is common in Hippocrates, fairly common in Herodotus, Plato, and Xenophon, unknown in the orators, Thucydides, and Aristotle. . . . It would appear that in post-Homeric Greek, at any rate in Attic, ἀτάρ was felt to be colloquial in tone, and was consequently avoided in formal language. Hence its frequency in Aristophanes, in Euripides (who aimed at realistic expression), and

[10] In a footnote at this point, Denniston compares "the narrow range of vocal inflexions used by an average speaker in the House of Commons with the numerous and subtle nuances employed on the Shakespearean stage and in everyday conversation." By comparison with the contemporary Reichstag, "average" speech in Commons might seem to resemble the most raucous bits of Shakespeare. My claim is that we cannot calibrate the style of the *genos dikanikon* by reference to professional speech alone, and that amateurs often went beyond even the looser and more dramatic parts of Demosthenes.

[11] Denniston dismisses ἤτοι at Lysias fr. 284 in Baiter and Sauppe's *Oratores Attici* as probably not part of Tzetzes' quotation.

in those prose-writers whose style approximates most closely to every-day conversation[12]

Two aspects of ἀτάρ are noteworthy. Its semantic force, particularly in Attic usage, is to mark "a break-off, a sudden change of topic" (52), and it is a particle given extra prominence by its invariable position as the initial word in a sentence or clause. I suggest that the professionals avoided the word because it risked dramatizing the speaker's astonishment or indecision in the midst of his utterance, perhaps brought on by a failure to prepare his speech adequately. ἀλλὰ μήν is common in the attested orators,[13] who (I think) heard the usage as allowing for a switch of topic, even to signal a presumably spontaneous idea,[14] while still marshalling a more dignified parade of assertions.

δή: "[I]n prose, especially the formal prose of history and oratory, there is a marked tendency to restrict emphatic δή to certain well-defined types of word" (204). For the use "with superlative adjectives and adverbs" (207) Denniston gives only one example from orators (Demosthenes 18.298, μεγίστων δὴ πραγμάτων, to which we can add Antiphon *Tetralogy* 1.42.1, καινότατα γὰρ δή). And "δή is freely used by the tragedians (perhaps too freely by Euripides) to emphasize verbs: not infrequently by Plato: and occasionally by other writers. In the austerer style of Thucydides and the orators this usage is hardly to be found" (214). Xenophon *The Education of Cyrus* 7.3.8 shows the flavor of this usage very clearly in Cyrus' words on seeing Abradatas' body and Panthea sitting beside it: Φεῦ, ὦ ἀγαθὴ καὶ πιστὴ ψυχή, οἴχη δὴ ἀπολιπὼν ἡμᾶς; ("Alas, dear heart, so good, so loyal; have you gone away[15] and left us?"). Admittedly, I have no examples with verbs to adduce from comedy, although we might think that the turn of phrase would have been an easy target for paratragedy.[16] But comedy is thick with this particle (there are some 350 instances), and I think it very likely that some amateur litigants, having very often heard δή used on the tragic stage to heighten pathos, reproduced the particular combination without noticing the professional's abstinence from it.

On ἦ μήν Denniston (350) writes that it "introduces a strong and confident asseveration, being used in both direct and indirect speech. It is most frequently employed in oaths and pledges: the wider use [i.e., *not* with

---

[12] Cf. López Eire 1996:131.

[13] Rough statistics: Andocides 2, Lysias 8, Isaeus 16, Isocrates 20, Demosthenes almost 90, Hyperides 5, Lycurgus 2.

[14] Whitehead ad Hyperides *Against Philippides* 5 (p. 56) nicely translates "It occurs to me."

[15] It would not be misleading to raise the heat of the translation to "Have you *really*. . . ." Xenophon's text recalls Aristophanes *Clouds* 719.

[16] Cf. Bers 1984:73 on the rarity of the terminal accusative in paratragedy.

oaths and pledges] is very rare in prose and entirely absent in the orators."
Denniston (351) gives five examples from orators, all clearly signaled as oaths,
and one from Plato's *Apology* (22a):

καὶ νὴ τὸν κύνα, ὦ ἄνδρες Ἀθηναῖοι – δεῖ γὰρ πρὸς ὑμᾶς τἀληθῆ
λέγειν – ἦ μὴν ἐγὼ ἔπαθόν τι τοιοῦτον·

By the dog, Athenian gentlemen – you see I must tell you the truth –
I swear something like this happened to me.[17]

Presumably *logographoi* were careful not to use ἦ μήν in a way that suggested
sloppiness in a legal matter. Amateur speakers were unlikely to be so
fastidious, and their usual linguistic habits[18] would put them at risk of seeming
too casual with oaths.

In his introduction to *The Greek Particles*, Denniston (lxxviii–lxxxii)
surveys a number of particle usages that appear peculiar to individual authors.
Antiphon's use of τοι and Lysias' predilection for καὶ μὲν δή have already
been mentioned. In the course of the book Denniston offers some remarks
on preferences shown by groups of orators, for example in choosing between
τοιγαροῦν and τοιγάρτοι (567). Most often it is Demosthenes who stands apart
from all the other canonical orators. Part of the explanation for his evidently
idiosyncratic and sometimes inconsistent taste in particles is certainly the size
of the Demosthenic corpus and the number of speeches possibly or certainly
written by others, in particular Apollodorus.[19] In some instances, however,
Denniston can attribute the stylistic turn to general features of Demosthenes'
style (lxxiv). For instance, connective ἄρα, which in Demosthenes always

---

[17] My translation strengthens the implicit reference to swearing.

[18] Think of the constantly interjected profanities and obscenities in English that many people
have difficulty in suppressing in contexts where they do the speaker harm.

[19] See Trevett 1992. Also, the corpus that has come to us under Demosthenes' name involves
an especially rich variety of rhetorical genres: no other corpus has the same wide-ranging
mix of forensic and ceremonial speeches. We cannot, for instance, contrast Aeschines' style
addressing the Ecclesia with his style addressing a *dikastêrion* hearing a routine, non-political
case, or Isaeus' epideictic manner with his forensic style. And it should be pointed out that
Denniston, a model of candor and careful exposition, admits his perplexity at some of his
findings. For instance, he observes that καὶ γάρ τοι is a combination "almost confined to
the Attic orators," whereas he lists no instances in attested oratory (and I can find none
either) of καὶ γὰρ οὖν; and he finds the semantics mysterious (113–114: but cf. MacDowell ad
Demosthenes 19.56, who is skeptical about the distinction Denniston sees between connective
and consequential meanings). Perhaps we are dealing with something of what might be called
a "Lieblingskombination" beloved by a few authors (I find seven examples in Lysias, ten in
Isocrates, twenty-three in Demosthenes, and one in Aeschines).

"has . . . a colloquial tone" (41), a fact that I suppose was enough to frighten off *logographoi* with a narrower range of colors on their palette. Demosthenes' pervasive liveliness of style explains why he favored the insertion of μέντοι with potential optatives "expressing lively surprise or indignation," a frequent usage in Aristophanes and Plato (402). I would guess that these two phenomena might, in fact, have been heard in amateur speech, at least when the speakers were accustomed to use phraseology more restrained than a flat-out indicative. In the case of corrective μὲν οὖν, which appear nowhere else in attested oratory, Denniston sees the usage as "characteristic of the dramatic vigour of Demosthenes' style that he, alone of the orators (except the authors of xxv and xliii, if he did not write those speeches), uses corrective μὲν οὖν" (479).[20] He gives five examples. We can be more specific: the dramatic quality is created by the orator (or an imitator whose work has intruded into the corpus) stopping in mid-sentence, as if interrupting himself with a thought that came to him just as he spoke. Indeed, that is the touch conveyed by Denniston's translation of 42.19, where the literal command to stop ("No, stop") is addressed to the clerk of the court, a transparent bit of simulated spontaneity.[21] Demosthenes' avoidance of three successive short syllables, in accordance with "Blass's law," is evidently the cause for his postponement of γε after disyllabic prepositions (148–149). Denniston makes it clear that he searched Demosthenes with particular attention for γε, but I think we would be on safe ground in assuming that it is very rare or nonexistent in the other attested orators. In this matter an *idiôtês* would have nothing to fear, since the word order that came naturally would set him apart only from Demosthenes.[22]

---

[20] Ever mindful of other hands at work in the Demosthenic corpus, Denniston notes that this use of the particle appears only in 25 and 43, both of uncertain authorship.

[21] On a similar allied phenomenon, Demosthenes' aversion to symmetry, and his occasional toleration of an Isocratean mannerism in μέν . . . δέ . . . constructions, see Denniston 1954:371. Also relevant: the collocation πῶς γὰρ οὔ; for "of course" (see Collard 2005:368), possibly a colloquialism. It is used a number of times by tragedians, and attested a few times in fourth-century comedy (Anaxandrides fr. 9 K-A, Antidotus fr. 3 K-A, and twice in Menander (*Dyscolus* 905, fr. 274 K-A). Demosthenes uses it three times in speeches he delivered himself (18.139, 299; 19.67).

[22] At Aeschines 3.117, the reported speech of a man described as disgusting and lacking cultivation includes the combination δέ γε in continuous speech, avoided by Isocrates as "too colloquial" (Denniston 1954:155): . . . ἀναβοήσας τις τῶν Ἀμφισσέων, ἄνθρωπος ἀσελγέστατος καὶ ὡς ἐμοὶ ἐφαίνετο οὐδεμιᾶς παιδείας μετεσχηκώς, ἴσως δὲ καὶ δαιμονίου τινὸς ἐξαμαρτάνειν προαγομένου, "ἀρχὴν δέ γε" ἔφη, "ὦ ἄνδρες Ἕλληνες, εἰ ἐσωφρονεῖτε, οὐδ' ἂν ὠνομάζετο τοὔνομα τοῦ δήμου τοῦ Ἀθηναίων ἐν ταῖσδε ταῖς ἡμέραις, ἀλλ' ὡς ἐναγεῖς ἐξείργετ' ἂν ἐκ τοῦ ἱεροῦ." (One of the Amphissaeans cried out. He was a thoroughly gross individual and, it seemed to me, a man with no education; perhaps, too, he was led into error by some superhuman force. He said: "Fellow Greeks, if you had any sense you would not mention the Athenian people at all during these days, but bar them from the temple as people under a curse.")

107

Denniston (383) offers a very interesting conjecture on stylistic pedagogy in the matter of one specific particle usage:

> The mock speeches in Aristophanes, modeled on the style of the assembly or the law-courts, almost always begin with μέν. . . . It is difficult to resist the impression that the budding speaker, at the turn of the fifth and fourth centuries, was recommended, as a kind of stylistic convention, to start off with a μέν, and to trust more or less to luck that he would find an answer to it, and not to care greatly if he did not. And this impression is strengthened by the prevalence of the μέν opening in contemporary oratory, Antiphon and Andocides.

Someone who was not a "budding speaker" might or might not have picked up this verbal tic. We have, then, a usage that an *idiôtês* might miss, and thereby demonstrate his lack of training; or he might try to imitate this feature in too obvious a manner, say by wearing a smug expression and looking around for his supporters to signal their admiration. Denniston's way of putting it suggests that the sequel to that opening particle was not of much importance, but the stylistic choices made by *logographoi* suggest they strove in particular to avoid uses with so strong a smell of the emotional, the diffident, or the colloquial as to mark the speaker as disrespectful of the state's judicial process. These *evitanda* are, I am arguing, precisely the pitfalls awaiting an *idiôtês* coming before an Athenian jury without the armor of a professionally written speech in his head or in his hands or, at a minimum, friends and relatives able to help him meet the challenge.

Oaths and Exclamations

No one who has read Old or New Comedy, satyr drama, Xenophon's *Memorabilia*, or even the austere language of Plato's *Laws* can doubt that Attic speakers, including those who might be thought to pride themselves on the "urbanity" of their speech, made frequent use of oaths and apostrophes, nearly all directed to a named or generic god or gods,[23] not for the practical purpose of

---

[23] Aeschines concludes his prosecution of Ctesiphon by calling on a mixture of heavenly bodies and abstractions (3.260): ἐγὼ μὲν οὖν, ὦ γῆ καὶ ἥλιε καὶ ἀρετὴ καὶ σύνεσις καὶ παιδεία, ᾗ διαγιγνώσκομεν τὰ καλὰ καὶ τὰ αἰσχρά . . . ("O earth and sun, virtue, intelligence, and education through which we distinguish what is noble and shameful . . ."; this is mocked by Demosthenes at 18.127). Demosthenes himself several times bursts out with "Oh, earth and gods!," a formula nowhere else attested (Kühnlein 1882:60).

binding themselves in a formal speech act, but to emphasize their words: νὴ Δία, μὰ τὸν Δία, πρὸς τῶν θεῶν, μὰ τοὺς θεούς, νὴ τὸν Ἡρακλέα καὶ πάντας θεός ("Yes, by Zeus!" "No, by Zeus!" "By the god!" "Yes, by Heracles and all the gods!"), and so on.[24] In tragedy there are few expressions that take this form (see below); remarkably enough, dicanic speech also generally abstained from this expressive element until Demosthenes and Aeschines. According to the statistics in Kühnlein 1882, Dover 1997:62, and my own searches, there are only a handful of examples in the first generation, and almost none are to be understood as the speaker's own declaration couched in the language he was using in court or even in the Assembly. One of the instances in Antiphon (fr. 70 Blass-Thalheim, quoted in the Suda) is interesting for its prominent position, evidently at the very opening of a speech written for a *graphê*:

ἐγραψάμην ταύτην τὴν γραφὴν ἠδικημένος ὑπὸ τούτου νὴ Δία πολλά, ἔτι δὲ καὶ πλείω ὑμᾶς ᾐσθημένος ἠδικημένους καὶ τοὺς ἄλλους πολίτας.

I have brought this public case because I was wronged by this man many times – by Zeus – and further because I perceived that you and the other citizens were wronged many more times.[25]

It may be significant that Antiphon relaxed his normal prosecutorial practice in a case that by category involved more than a single individual, and that he makes his claim that many others in the city were also victims: the wholesale change seen in Demosthenes might be a symptom of the same phenomenon.

At Andocides 3 *On the Peace*, a symbouleutic speech, the oath falls within an imaginary dialogue (3.15):

ἀλλὰ νὴ Δία ἕως ἂν Λακεδαιμονίους καταπολεμήσωμεν καὶ τοὺς συμμάχους αὐτῶν, μέχρι τούτου δεῖ πολεμεῖν; ἀλλ᾽ οὔ μοι δοκοῦμεν οὕτω παρεσκευάσθαι. ἐὰν δ᾽ ἄρα κατεργασώμεθα, τί ποτε αὐτοὶ πείσεσθαι δοκοῦμεν ὑπὸ τῶν βαρβάρων, ὅταν ταῦτα πράξωμεν;

MacDowell's translation uses quotations marks to signal the imaginary change of speaker: "But we must go on fighting until we've beaten the Spartans and their allies"; "But I don't think we're equipped for that; and if we do

---

[24] A locus classicus for oaths filling the air at marketplaces: Cyrus quoted at Herodotus 1.153.

[25] Dover 1997:62 overlooks the oath at Antiphon 6.40, ὦ Ζεῦ καὶ θεοὶ πάντες, which Blass 1887–98:1.203 calls an instance of a lively figure "in the manner of Demosthenes." There may be another oath at fr. 1b1, μὰ τοὺς θεοὺς τοὺς Ὀλυμπίους, but the text is too wretched to allow certainty.

accomplish it, what do you think the barbarians will do to us in our turn when we've done it?"[26]

The Lysianic corpus has no oaths whatever, unless we count *Against Andocides*, a speech almost certainly from a different hand.[27]

Dover 1997:62[28] regards oaths as an "informal" feature, citing "their absence from tragedy . . . but presence in satyr-plays (six times in Eur[ipides] *Cyclops*) and in dipinti (Θέογνις καλὸς νὴ Δία on a black-figure cup from Palermo . . .)," and their distribution elsewhere in literature. For Dover, the quite sudden increase in the use of oaths, first in Isaeus, and then in Demosthenes, corroborates his classification of oaths as "informal." He characterizes these "informal" oaths as "casual" and "serving as intensification." As I remark in discussing his treatment of the deictic iota in the Appendix, I do not believe the term satisfactory.

The comparison with tragic usage is problematic. Dover's very low numbers seem to me an epiphenomenon of the worldview presupposed in the plays. The immanence, or even direct representation, of gods makes a crucial difference. It is one thing to swear by an Olympian while buying or selling fish ("By Poseidon, you won't get an obol out of me for these stinking mullets!"); it is another if the conceptual world of the speaker conventionally portrays those gods and anthropomorphized abstractions as potential or actualized players in the unfolding action. Obviously Clytemnestra cannot be said to be using a "casual" oath, one merely "serving as intensification," when she solemnizes her claim of fearfulness by invoking the very powers she claims to have propitiated by murdering her husband.[29] Even the specific utterance in Euripides that Dover singles out as "the nearest thing in tragedy to the casual oath of prose dialogue" (1997:62) fails to meet his specification: an oath by "my lady," that is, Hera. This deity is one most Greek women would think emotionally and intellectually connected to the very subject of discussion, protecting a marriage from disruption, and tragic playwrights routinely

---

[26] For oaths in *hypophorai* see Bers 1997:195–196.

[27] There are three examples in *Against Andocides*, an amateurish job that nearly all agree was not written by Lysias himself (see Dover 1968b passim, and the introduction to Todd 2000).

[28] His earlier statement on the question: Dover 1985:328 (reprinted in 1987:48).

[29] Aeschylus *Agamemnon* 1431–1434:

καὶ τήνδ' ἀκούεις ὁρκίων ἐμῶν θέμιν· | μὰ τὴν τέλειον τῆς ἐμῆς παιδὸς Δίκην, | Ἄτην Ἐρινύν θ', αἷσι τόνδ' ἔσφαξ' ἐγώ, | οὔ μοι Φόβου μέλαθρον ἐλπὶς ἐμπατεῖ . . .

(You hear also the rightness of my oath: By my daughter's Justice that brings fulfillment, and by her *Atê* [agent of ruin] and Erinys, for whom I slaughtered this man, no fearful expectation walks in this palace.)

present the gods as interested in the unfolding action.[30] Moreover, tragic characters inhabit a world of great deeds and great sufferings, and they express themselves in a highly artificial, largely traditional language, into which colloquialisms were introduced sparingly (even by Euripides). Strong affect is, as it were, the assumed background of a language – spoken and sung – likely to resist a quotidian means of signaling affect. Tragic language was formal *and* affective.

The absence of oaths in public speech related by Thucydides and Xenophon is also less significant than Dover thinks. Even if speakers did swear in the course of their forensic and political speeches, Thucydides would not have been likely to reveal that fact to us. Oaths convey the sort of naturalism in the depiction of human actions for which he had little use. When he chooses to mention strong emotion, his description is expressed abstractly, deals mostly with groups, and is spare in its details.[31] Xenophon, as Dover remarks, deploys oaths mostly in the representation of dialogue,[32] but this is a fact of uncertain significance. Compared to the speeches in Thucydides, those in the *Hellenica* appear more in line with our notions of conventional rhetoric, but not more credible as accurate documents of the actual texts.

Though neither father or son is a litigant in the mock trial of Labes the dog in the *Wasps*, both men are excited. Philocleon interrupts the dog-prosecutor's speech to express his wholehearted confirmation of the charge of cheese-stealing (912–914):

νὴ τὸν Δί', ἀλλὰ δῆλός ἐστ'· ἔμοιγέ τοι
τυροῦ κάκιστον ἀρτίως ἐνήρυγεν
ὁ βδελυρὸς οὗτος.

By Zeus, he did it, plain as day. This filthy dog just let rip the most awful cheesy belch at me!

---

[30] Euripides *Andromache* 934. The oath is in fact nested within a piece of *oratio recta*, but tragedy almost never uses this device to introduce linguistic features excluded from the basic language of the genre: see Bers 1997:50, 63n73, 71.

[31] Two famous instances: the herald stunned by the calamity at 4.101 (Stahl 1966:134–136; Stahl 2003:133–135), and the swaying of Athenians' bodies as they looked out on the confusing and changing battle in the harbor at Syracuse, 7.71.3. Thucydides' reporting of dialogue, where he might have allowed an oath, is exceedingly spare (Bers 1997:222n10). And readers will not need to be reminded that the fidelity of his speeches to the original, or even whether all of the speeches he reports took place, is a matter of perennial controversy.

[32] Dover identifies only two that serve as Xenophon's "intensification of his own statement" (1997:62)."

Bdelycleon remonstrates with his father (919–920):

πρὸς τῶν θεῶν, μὴ προκαταγίγνωσκ᾽, ὦ πάτερ,
πρὶν ἄν γ᾽ ἀκούσῃς ἀμφοτέρων.

By the gods, Dad, don't convict him before you've heard both sides!

And just as the prosecuting dog sums up and takes his seat, Philocleon is quite beside himself (931–934):

ἰοὺ ἰού.
ὅσας κατηγόρησε τὰς πανουργίας.
κλέπτον τὸ χρῆμα τἀνδρός. οὐ καὶ σοὶ δοκεῖ,
ὦ 'λεκτρυών; νὴ τὸν Δί᾽ ἐπιμύει γέ τοι.

Wow! What a pile of crimes he's denounced! Here's a lump of larceny don't you think, Rooster? By Zeus, the rooster's winking "Yes"!

The prosecutor knows to avoid these exclamations; the defendant can, in any event, only say "Bow!" and hope the parade of his pups will mollify the one-man jury played by Philocleon. Real speakers – impatient, indignant, frightened – probably were not always so restrained. Even *logographoi* might break out with an utterance, not even a word in the standard sense, suggesting triumph or despair, but only Demosthenes dared leave one in a published text, and even he identified the cry as not precisely his alone. Once it is a sort of moan (in translation I use the inadequate "Oh!")[33] his enemies' politics inspire in brave men (23.210):

καίτοι πηλίκον τί ποτ᾽ ἄν στενάξειαν οἱ ἄνδρες ἐκεῖνοι, οἱ ὑπὲρ δόξης καὶ ἐλευθερίας τελευτήσαντες, καὶ πολλῶν καὶ καλῶν ἔργων ὑπομνήματα καταλιπόντες, εἰ ἄρ᾽ αἴσθοινθ᾽ ὅτι νῦν ἡ πόλις εἰς ὑπηρέτου σχῆμα καὶ τάξιν προελήλυθεν, καὶ Χαρίδημον εἰ χρὴ φρουρεῖν βουλεύεται; Χαρίδημον; οἴμοι.

But how loudly would those men who died for the city's good name and freedom and left memorials of their many brave acts cry out if they saw that our city has now sunk to the crouching posture and station of a slave, and that we deliberate whether we must guard Charidemus? *Charidemus?* Oh!

---

[33] If it were not an archaism, I would have used "Woe is me!" And it did not risk provoking an out-of-place laugh at an apparent Yiddishism, I would have used a word that exactly duplicates the sound of the Greek word: "Oy!"

In Isaeus things begin to change: there are 15 instances according to Kühnlein, 14 by Dover's count. Dionysius of Halicarnassus remarks that Isaeus was a transitional figure in the history of oratory,[34] and although Dionysius does not say so, I believe that the transition he effected was, in part, the introduction into the *genos dikanikon* of the more flamboyant style of the *rhêtores* who made frequent appearances in the Ecclesia. We then have comparatively large numbers for Aeschines (39 according to Kühnlein) and some 300 in Demosthenes. But even then, most of these oaths are not interjections that manifest the speaker's emotion, but rather occur within the introductions that frame stretches of hypothetical speech attributed to persons other than the speaker (see Dover 1997:62–63). And there are only a few instances of oaths starting μά or νή in the latest orators of the Canon (Dinarchus, Hyperides, and Lycurgus).

Further, within the Demosthenic corpus, oaths are more common in the public than the private speeches. Blass 1887–98:3.1:83 remarks that "rhetorical vivacity and power" have more scope in the former than the latter and that earlier oratory was spare in the use of such expression, and also that in those private speeches he regarded as authentic invective is more restrained than in the pseudodemosthenic speeches.[35]

What I believe is missing from Dover's treatment of oaths is precisely what he has pretty much excluded by his definition – an acknowledgment of their fundamentally affective flavor. When used in the circumstances of a speech that, at the very least, dictated a particular physical situation, an order of speakers, and signals to start (if not also to stop), even a mode of emphasizing words could – I believe often did – suggest an overly excitable, hence contemptible, personality.

What needs to be added, then, is that oaths, like curses and name-calling, are at the same time blatantly affective and exceedingly vulgar, in the literal meaning of the word. They are instruments of verbal aggression or expressions of strong emotion that issue naturally from a man under duress expressing himself without regard to the circumstances in which he is speaking. I believe the professionals understood that such language did not on its own persuade

---

[34] Isaeus 3.3.13: πηγή τις ὄντως ἐστὶ τῆς Δημοσθένους δυνάμεως ("the real spring from which the rhetorical power of Demosthenes flows") and 3.24–25: μεταβολαῖς ἐναγωνίων καὶ παθητικῶν ποικίλλει τοὺς λόγους ("he carries the development of his arguments to great length and gives variety to his speeches by alternating devices of debate with emotional appeal"; both in Usher's translation).

[35] Blass on the same page compares Demosthenes' restraint to the strict ban on mentioning aspects of daily life observed by French poets of his own era. Cf. Kühnlein 1882:60–61.

113

those who – an important qualification – did not already stand with the man who mouthed them. On the contrary, they suggested a character likely to look exclusively to his own interests, the sort of man Athenians assembled in juries were not prone to favor. On the other hand, starting at least with Antiphon, an oath might be acceptable in a context where the emotion was not exclusively the speaker's own, but attributed to others or shared with the *dêmos* – or so the speaker hoped.

οὐ μή

Dicanic speech is full of denials and prohibitions, and the palette of posthomeric Greek syntax is rich in ways of expressing these notions, among them οὐ μή with the future indicative or a subjunctive, predominantly in the aorist, carrying the nuance "in no way whatsoever" (Goodwin 1890: §295; Wackernagel 1928).[36]

We meet many examples of the construction in tragedy and comedy, but also in speeches in historiography and in Plato. The tone is unquestionably emphatic. These few examples are characteristic:

Aristophanes *Birds* 460–462:

᾿Αλλ᾽ ἐφ᾽ ὅτῳπερ πράγματι τὴν σὴν ἥκεις γνώμην ἀναπείσας,
λέγε θαρρήσας· ὡς τὰς σπονδὰς οὐ μὴ πρότερον παραβῶμεν. [37]

Come, tell what's the purpose for which you've come to win us over to your opinion. Don't be scared; tell us. Understand, *we* will not be the first to break the truce.

Two battlefield exhortations in Thucydides involve vehement denials that there will be invasions. The first is direct speech (4.95.2), the second is a clause within *oratio obliqua* (5.69.2):

. . . ὑπὲρ τῆς ἡμετέρας ὁ ἀγὼν ἔσται· καὶ ἢν νικήσωμεν, οὐ μή ποτε ὑμῖν Πελοποννήσιοι ἐς τὴν χώραν ἄνευ τῆς τῶνδε ἵππου ἐσβάλωσιν.

---

[36] The same syntactical form is used by tragic and comic poets for prohibitions in the second-person singular, but there are to my knowledge no prose attestations whatsoever (Kühner-Gerth 1898–1904:2.222–223; Goodwin 1890: §297). Exclusion from prose suggests a construction with a very strong flavor indeed, even granted the rarity of addresses in that person and number. Chronological pride of place apparently belongs to Parmenides 2.7.1 DK: οὐ γὰρ μήποτε τοῦτο δαμῆι εἶναι μὴ ἐόντα.

[37] I have seen no attestations of the construction in Aristophanes' fourth-century plays.

The stakes of this battle will be our territory; and if we win, the Peloponnesians *will not*, without [the Boeotian cavalry] invade our land.

... οὐ μὴ ποτέ τις αὐτοῖς ἄλλος ἐς τὴν γῆν ἔλθῃ.

... no one else will *ever* launch an attack on their territory.[38]

Plato uses the construction for Socrates' manifesto (*Apology* 29d4–5):

ἕωσπερ ἂν ἐμπνέω καὶ οἷός τε ὦ, οὐ μὴ παύσωμαι φιλοσοφῶν ...

As long as I breathe and it is in my power, I will *not* stop doing philosophy ...

Most striking is an appearance of the construction in the generally bloodless speech of the *Laws*. At 942c5–d3 the Athenian stranger speaks of the necessity for group obedience in military organizations:

τούτου γὰρ οὔτ' ἔστιν οὔτε ποτὲ μὴ γένηται κρεῖττον οὔτε ἄμεινον οὔτε τεχνικώτερον εἰς σωτηρίαν τὴν κατὰ πόλεμον καὶ νίκην – τοῦτο ἐν εἰρήνῃ μελετητέον εὐθὺς ἐκ τῶν παίδων, ἄρχειν τε ἄλλων ἄρχεσθαί θ' ὑφ' ἑτέρων·

A wiser and better rule than this man neither has discovered, nor ever will, nor a truer art of military salvation and victory. 'Tis this lesson of commanding our fellows and being commanded by them we should rehearse in the times of peace, from our very cradles.

(Trans. A. E. Taylor)[39]

The construction persists into New Comedy, as at Menander *Samia* 428, where an impatient character complains οὐ μὴ δύῃ ποθ' ἥλιος· ("The sun will *never* go down!").

Yet this mode is hardly to be found in the Canon of Attic Orators, even if we go outside the *genos dikanikon* and include the political speeches, the

---

[38] In a speech at Xenophon *Anabasis* 6.2.4, the construction occurs at a tense moment: ἀναστὰς δὲ Λύκων Ἀχαιὸς εἶπε· Θαυμάζω μέν, ὦ ἄνδρες, τῶν στρατηγῶν ὅτι οὐ πειρῶνται ἡμῖν ἐκπορίζειν σιτηρέσιον· τὰ μὲν γὰρ ξένια οὐ μὴ γένηται τῇ στρατιᾷ τριῶν ἡμερῶν σιτία. ...

[39] It seems appropriate in this instance to use an archaic-sounding translation to suggest the gravity of the pronouncement.

dêmêgoriai.[40] What is almost certainly our earliest example appears in a speech delivered sometime after the first decade of the fourth century (the terminus post quem is 383, the ante quem 363: see Wyse 1904:588), a vehement prohibition at Isaeus 8.24.1:

κaίτοι εἰ μὴ ἦν θυγατριδοῦς Κίρωνος, οὐκ ἂν ταῦτα διωμολογεῖτο, ἀλλ᾽ ἐκείνους ἂν τοὺς λόγους ἔλεγε· "Σὺ δὲ τίς εἶ; Σοὶ δὲ τί προσήκει θάπτειν; Οὐ γιγνώσκω σε· οὐ μὴ εἰσίῃς εἰς τὴν οἰκίαν."

And yet if I'd not been Ciron's grandson, he would never have made these arrangements but would have said, "Who are you? What gives you the right to bury him? I don't know you; you're not going to set foot in the house."

But this is imagined speech, words that the speaker' opponent, whose estate is under dispute, *might* have said under other circumstances. Most significantly, the negative command is not what would have been said in court, but in a private conversation, hence it is not strictly part of forensic speech (Bers 1997:141).[41]

All of the other examples I am aware of come from the corpora of Aeschines and Demosthenes. At [Demosthenes] 53.8 *Against Nicostratus*, a speech pretty certainly written by the prosecutor, Apollodorus, for his own use, he says that he had once pitied Nicostratus, having seen the scars he carried from fetters he wore when captured and held in slavery:

καὶ ἅμα ὁρῶν κακῶς διακείμενον καὶ δεικνύοντα ἕλκη ἐν ταῖς κνήμαις ὑπὸ δεσμῶν, ὧν ἔτι τὰς οὐλὰς ἔχει, καὶ ἐὰν κελεύσητε αὐτὸν δεῖξαι, οὐ μὴ 'θελήσῃ ...

I felt pity for him when I heard this and saw the wounds left by the chains on his shanks, where I saw there were still scars – though if you ask him to show you the scars, he certainly will refuse to do it.

It is very much in the speaker's interests to present the defendant as pitiable in a bad sense. Part of that strategy – or perhaps simple exploitation of the facts – involves mentioning that Nicostratus was lachrymose during their

---

[40] A confession: the list I give at Bers 1997:141 with n38 misses a few examples with compounded negatives, falsely lists Aeschines 3.177 as 1.177, and should not have referred to Demosthenes 44.7.

[41] Bekker reads the future indicative, εἴσει, an emendation not germane to the question of provenance.

meeting (§7: κλάων) and bears disfiguring marks that he will refuse to display, even if the jury asks him to, presumably from fear that the sight will trigger the jurors' instinctive contempt for a body made ugly by servile labor. We might say that Apollodorus wants the jury to imagine the fierce obstinacy with which the defendant would refuse the request he is, in effect, trying to incite.

The remaining examples are from speeches that are either symbouleutic or, in the case of Aeschines' prosecution of Ctesiphon and Demosthenes' response, tightly bound to a political struggle and therefore symbouleutic in content, though not occasion. In the *First Philippic* Demosthenes emphasizes the danger of mutual recriminations.[42] Similarly, at the close of the *Third Philippic* Demosthenes warns against individual Athenians looking to others for help, rather than acting themselves.[43] In the *Second Philippic* he says that mistrust is democracy's shield against tyrants.[44] Likewise, Aeschines, in his speech prosecuting Ctesiphon for alleged illegalities in his motion to present Demosthenes for his public service, warns the jury that by recklessly bestowing awards on politicians they will "never makes rogues honest, but . . . will reduce decent men to utter despair" (3.177).[45] In *On the Crown*, technically a defense of Ctesiphon, Demosthenes claims that anyone inquiring into all the actions for which a politician is held to account will find that he did all he should have.[46]

The οὐ μή construction is more restrained than curses, but shares their excessively affective quality. On οὐ μή I adduce a piece of characteristically pungent Gildersleeve (1902:137–138):

> οὐ μή belongs to the dialogue of the wrangling mart; it belongs to the drama, by which, it would seem, so many vulgarities have found their way into classic society. . . . History has no need of it [i.e. in narrative: but see examples from speeches in Thucydides and Xenophon above] and the orators use it sparingly. The elevation of the bema carried with it certain conventionalities which even common creatures like

---

[42] 1.44–45: ἤρετό τις. εὑρήσει τὰ σαθρά, ὦ ἄνδρες Ἀθηναῖοι, τῶν ἐκείνου πραγμάτων αὐτὸς ὁ πόλεμος, ἂν ἐπιχειρῶμεν· ἂν μέντοι καθώμεθ' οἴκοι, λοιδορουμένων ἀκούοντες καὶ αἰτιωμένων ἀλλήλους τῶν λεγόντων, οὐδέποτ' οὐδὲν ἡμῖν μὴ γένηται τῶν δεόντων.

[43] 3.75: εἰ δ' ὃ βούλεται ζητῶν ἕκαστος καθεδεῖται, καὶ ὅπως μηδὲν αὐτὸς ποιήσει σκοπῶν, πρῶτον μὲν οὐδὲ μήποθ' εὕρῃ τοὺς ποιήσοντας, ἔπειτα δέδοιχ' ὅπως μὴ πάνθ' ἅμ' ὅσ' οὐ βουλόμεθα ποιεῖν ἡμῖν ἀνάγκη γενήσεται.

[44] 6.24, grammatically a denial, but rhetorically closer to an assertion: ταύτην [ἀπιστίαν] φυλάττετε, ταύτης ἀντέχεσθε· ἂν ταύτην σώζητε, οὐδὲν μὴ δεινὸν πάθητε.

[45] τοὺς μὲν γὰρ πονηροὺς οὐ μή ποτε βελτίους ποιήσετε, τοὺς δὲ χρηστοὺς εἰς τὴν ἐσχάτην ἀθυμίαν ἐμβαλεῖτε.

[46] 18.246: οὐδεὶς μήποθ' εὕρῃ κατ' ἔμ' οὐδὲν ἐλλειφθέν.

Aeschines . . . had to respect. "Keep your hand snugly within your himation [cloak]," said to himself the ex-actor. . . . "Don't point. Don't fling about your articular proper nouns. Don't make free with οὐ μή." Why, even Demosthenes, who dared everything, is shy of it, and his master Isaios uses it once only, and then in one of those dramatic bits[47] that help to make us understand how he was the fountain of the power of Demosthenes. Turn to the LXX, turn to the New Testament, and in half an hour you will gather up more οὐ μή's than are to be found in all classic literature. It has become the cheap emphasis of a showy race and a degenerate time.

Given the pattern of usage, which includes tragic language and even presocratic poetry (Parmenides: see Collard 2005:378), Gildersleeve cannot be correct in characterizing the construction as a "vulgarity"; and the moralizing peroration tells us more about his social and ethnic views than about Greek. Still, he does seem to have caught the flavor of οὐ μή accurately enough: it is an expression that suggests the speaker raises his voice, or even stamps his foot, and that suggests a level of affect the skilled forensic speaker would work to avoid.

σφόδρα

Genre-conditioning may apply not only to lexicon, but to word order. The adverb σφόδρα, found in virtually every genre of Greek literature,[48] appears to be used in a position relative to pause – roughly, the spots punctuated in our texts – that vary with stylistic level. It has long been noticed that the adverb σφόδρα tends to gravitate to verse-final position in comedy: even LSJ, a work that usually takes no notice of word order, remarks on that fact (s.v.).[49] Plato has some thirty examples of σφόδρα immediately before a strong pause, most

---

[47] Gildersleeve's reference is to one of only two pieces of *oratio recta* in Isaeus (Bers 1997:141).

[48] Though only rarely in tragedy. Dover 1985:335n41 reports only two attestations in Sophocles, one in the tragic *adespota*, and one in a satyr play.

[49] Dover offers a more refined analysis. He observes that "[i]n positive clauses in which it intensifies an adjacent M [mobile] comedy has a certain preference for putting the intensified M . . . first and σφόδρα . . . second" (1985:335), a fact that would on its own favor a concentration of the word at verse-final position (σφόδρα postponed to the next line would require overcoming a general resistance to enjambment). In prose, on the other hand, σφόδρα has an even stronger tendency to *precede* the mobile, and in some instances the word seems "to impart an oath-like affirmative charge to the whole sentence"; he gives Lysias 12.63 as an example (1985:336).

in a few set phrases like πάνυ σφόδρα.[50] In the orators, however, in whom the word occurs about 140 times, there are only two examples of the word so placed, both in Lysias, both in prosecution speeches:

13.13: . . . καὶ ἄλλοι τινὲς τῶν πολιτῶν εὐνοοῦντες ὑμῖν, ὥς γ᾽ ἐδή-
λωσεν ὕστερον, ἠγανάκτουν σφόδρα.

. . . and several other citizens who supported you, as they later showed – went to see him and protested vigorously.

14.27:[51] ὁ δὲ πατὴρ αὐτὸν οὕτως ἐμίσει σφόδρα, ὥστ᾽ οὐδ᾽ <ἂν> ἀπο-
θανόντος ἔφασκε τὰ ὀστᾶ κομίσασθαι.

. . . his father hated him so much that he declared he would not even collect his bones if he died.

The rarity of σφόδρα before a pause does not look like an accident. My guess is that σφόδρα in that position was fairly common in excited colloquial speech and became an *evitandum* in professional writing because its rhythm was associated with overwrought vehemence, something like a speaker tacking on a "No, really!" after each of his assertions because he feels very little confidence in his rhetoric.

Diminutives

Hypocoristic (endearing) and pejorative or deteriorative (condemning) diminutives are affective by their very nature. Compared to many other languages, contemporary English is impoverished in this part of lexicon, but Italian (among others) is rich in productive suffixes in this category: *Topolino* (Mickey Mouse's Italian name) is an example of the former, *Vittoriaccio* (bad Victor) of the latter. (As they are not similarly affective, the "faded"

---

[50] Of these, the only ones attributed to Socrates are: after a full stop one (out of a total of nine) at *Alcibiades I* 124d3, a dialogue of controversial authenticity; two after a comma (out of a total of nineteen, including four in the *Laws* and one each in the presumably spurious *Letters* and the *Eryxias*) at *Phaedrus* 254c1 and *Lysis* 212a4; one after a question mark (out of a total of one) at *Theaetetus* 152a9; and none (out of a total of zero) after a half-stop. Perhaps Plato gave Socrates a fastidious reluctance to placing σφόδρα in a "vulgar" position. Of course, it is mostly Socrates' interlocutors who respond with πάνυ σφόδρα or πάνυ γε σφόδρα, and Socrates is not present in the *Laws*.

[51] This speech against the son of Alcidiades was delivered to a jury of soldiers.

diminutives, like Latin *puella*, from *puer*, are irrelevant.)[52] Aristotle discusses diminutives at *Rhetoric* 1405b28–34:

> ἔστιν αὖ τὸ ὑποκορίζεσθαι· ἔστιν δὲ ὁ ὑποκορισμὸς ὃ ἐλαττονποιεῖ
> καὶ τὸ κακὸν καὶ τὸ ἀγαθόν, ὥσπερ καὶ Ἀριστοφάνης σκώπτει ἐν
> τοῖς Βαβυλωνίοις, ἀντὶ μὲν χρυσίου χρυσιδάριον, ἀντὶ δ' ἱματίου
> ἱματιδάριον, ἀντὶ δὲ λοιδορίας λοιδορημάτιον καὶ ἀντὶ νοσήματος
> νοσημάτιον. εὐλαβεῖσθαι δὲ δεῖ καὶ παρατηρεῖν ἐν ἀμφοῖν τὸ
> μέτριον.

The same effect [of attributing goodness or badness, beauty or ugliness] can be achieved by diminution. A diminutive [*hypokorismos*] makes both bad and good less so, as Aristophanes does sarcastically in the *Babylonians* when he substitutes *goldlet* for *gold*, *cloaklet* for *cloak*, *insultlet* for *insult*, and *diseaselet* [for *disease*]. But one should be careful and observe moderation in both [epithets and diminutives].

(Trans. Kennedy 1991)

It is not surprising that Aristotle's examples are all taken from Old Comedy, for it is the only genre of Greek literature in which diminutives can be found with any frequency. In this stylistic feature the canonical Attic orators certainly did observe Aristotle's strictures: there are a handful in those preserved forensic speeches with an obvious political agenda, but elsewhere the speechwriters' moderation amounts very nearly to total abstinence.

In the court speeches involving political figures, however, we meet some colorful diminutives. Andocides 1.130 has diminutive forms for 'children' and 'women' (*paidaria*, *gunaia*) but as generic terms only the second can count as intrinsically contemptuous, since a very small child (the diminutive is strengthened by the adjective *mikrotata*) cannot be expected to understand

---

[52] Petersen 1910:125 (cf. 131, tentatively extending the claim to ἱμάτιον) categorizes as deteriorative ληκύθιον at Demosthenes 24.114, translating it as "worthless bottle." The sentence runs: καὶ εἴ τίς γ' ἐκ Λυκείου ἢ ἐξ Ἀκαδημείας ἢ ἐκ Κυνοσάργους ἱμάτιον ἢ ληκύθιον ἢ ἄλλο τι φαυλότατον, ἢ εἰ τῶν σκευῶν τι τῶν ἐκ τῶν γυμνασίων ὑφέλοιτο ἢ ἐκ τῶν λιμένων, ὑπὲρ δέκα δραχμάς, καὶ τούτοις θάνατον ἐνομοθέτησεν εἶναι τὴν ζημίαν. Though the repeated ending -ιον might play an acoustic part in the contemptuous description of petty crimes that would merit execution, it is very unlikely that the jurors would think of ληκύθιον as anything but an oil-flask.

the matter at hand.[53] Aristogeiton, the butt of Demosthenes 25, is an active public speaker (his supporters, the speaker says, style him the "watchdog of the democracy" [§40]). At §57 the speaker applies *gunaion* to an alien woman with whom Aristogeiton has consorted (and then abused). She is introduced into his narrative by name (Zobia), which is in itself a mark of disrespect (Schaps 1977). The narrative makes it clear that she is to be taken as possessing shameful qualities no juror would want attributed to his own mother or sister. Another pejorative in -ιον is practically swallowed up in the dense barrage of abuse (see Usher 1993 and Yunis 2001 for analysis) that Demosthenes fires at Aeschines in *On the Crown* 242:

πονηρόν, ἄνδρες Ἀθηναῖοι, πονηρὸν ὁ συκοφάντης ἀεὶ καὶ παν-
ταχόθεν βάσκανον καὶ φιλαίτιον· τοῦτο δὲ καὶ φύσει κίναδος τἀν-
θρώπιόν ἐστιν, οὐδὲν ἐξ ἀρχῆς ὑγιὲς πεποιηκὸς οὐδ᾽ ἐλεύθερον,
αὐτοτραγικὸς πίθηκος, ἀρουραῖος Οἰνόμαος, παράσημος ῥήτωρ.

Every sycophant is a depraved character, depraved as well as back-stabbing and faultfinding at every opportunity; and this *puny fellow* is by nature a rogue. From the beginning he's done nothing useful or generous. He's a real ape on the tragic stage, an Oenomaus of the countryside, a counterfeit politician.

Wankel 1976 remarks that this is the sole instance of the word ἀνθρώπιον securely attested within a speech.[54] In *On the Crown* Demosthenes uses the word *graidion* ("old hag") at §260 and at §261 *arkhidion* for a contemptibly low public office once discharged by Aeschines. In *Against the Sophists*, a work normally categorized as a sort of pamphlet, Isocrates uses λογίδια to refer to the theories of competitors who have claimed to offer instruction useful for the composition of lawcourt speeches, but to my knowledge there are no diminutives in any of Isocrates' few actual forensic compositions (13.20).

Petersen is certainly right to insist that one cannot be certain a priori that a word that by morphology could be taken as a diminutive carried any

---

[53] *Pace* MacDowell 1962 and Edwards 1995 ad loc. MacDowell 1998 translates: ". . . you all know that tiny children and silly [Edwards has "weak"] women all through the city used to tell a tale that Hipponicus kept a devil inside his house, who upturned his table [*trapedza*, the word also used for 'bank']."

[54] It occurs in the description of Demosthenes himself attributed to Demades fr. 89 de Falco: συγκείμενον ἀνθρώπιον [if we follow the text found in Tzetzes, instead of ἀνθρωπάριον] ἐκ συλλαβῶν καὶ γλώττης, but as Wankel notes, this "is not from a speech, or at least not from an authentic speech"; and in Tzetzes there is a variant (ἀνθρώπιον).

positive or negative connotations in a particular passage.[55] Still, we can some-times be all but certain. No one will be surprised that orators abstain from *dikastêridion*, a word used by Aristophanes at *Wasps* 803 to refer to the liter-ally miniature court Philocleon imagines could be established in front of every Athenian's house. Even if the meaning were free of condescending or dismis-sive connotations, a speaker who possessed even a minimum degree of tact would understand that anything that could be construed as insulting the body charged with judging his case had to be avoided. At *Knights* 347 Aristophanes has the diminutive *dikidion*, "trifling law case." A speaker might use the word to refer contemptuously to a case other than the one at hand, say a suit his opponent had initiated on some other occasion. But *dikidion* could, I imagine, offend some jurors who regarded the adjudication of even the smallest disputes that came before the *dikastêria* as intrinsic to the democracy. But it is not obvious why Lysias decided against having his client speaking in a *doki-masia* before the Council (Lysias 24) use the word *arguridion* ("a bit of money," in older English perhaps "a farthing" or "ha'penny"), a diminutive attested in Aristophanes (*Wealth* 240, fr. 547 K-A). Lysias' client is arguing that he is enti-tled by virtue of his disability to receive the city's indeed very small one-obol daily welfare payment, and his tone is plainly jocular at times, for instance when he complains that the prosecutor is treating the case as if the estate of an heiress was at stake (§14).

Given that affective diminutives are attested in reasonably large numbers only in comedy, we cannot be sure that they played an important role in the routine speech, even of Athenians in the grip of emotion. Nevertheless, I hazard the guess that they would not be so rare in professional speech if they were not at the very least an affective resource perceived by *logographoi* as the sort of thing an amateur had to be advised to leave behind when he stepped up to the *bêma*. Demosthenes did use deterioratives in some memorable passages, but as we have seen in the discussion of several other linguistic features, his own de facto political speeches deviated markedly from the forensic norm.

Repetition

Aside from shaking the fist, shouting, and the like, repeating one's words is probably the most primitive and most common form of raising the temperature of one's speech – in any language. The earliest attested example

---

[55] Petersen 1910:128–129, with reference specifically to possible deteriorative meaning in words ending in -ιον.

of repeated words in literary Greek[56] is Aphrodite's doubled vocative, "Ares, Ares" (*Iliad* 5.31) as she wheedles him into withdrawal from battle.[57] Some artful forms of repetition,[58] for instance anaphora and antistrophe, are well-known elements of the *technê rhêtorikê*, though they can be called frequent only in Lysias and Demosthenes. As it can be assumed that these were not part of routine speech, they are not important to my argument. Also irrelevant to this discussion are repetitions in sacral formulae[59] and "repetition for the sake of clearness" (Denniston 1952:92–98). The pertinent form is an exact and immediate, or almost immediate, repetition. I exclude, of course, "expressive gemination" of the sort that has been permanently built into words, as in the reduplication of perfective verbs. In rhetorical jargon, the best term is *epanadiplosis*, as defined by Denniston 1952:90–91: "the simple doubling of a word for the sake of emphasis." The emphasis might serve a sort of ritual certainty with an emotional charge, as at Aristophanes *Frogs* 305–306 ("Swear it!") or more generally "to mark the speaker's agitation" (Olson ad Aristophanes *Acharnians* 280–283, among the examples cited by Denniston).[60]

The surprising thing is that epanadiplosis is very rare in dicanic speech, whether in the simplest forms where the word is repeated without any interruption, or in more complex structures.[61] Denniston finds it in only in Aeschines ("very occasionally"), Demosthenes, and, with the greatest frequency, Dinarchus, the "gingerbread Demosthenes" as Denniston calls him, following Hermogenes (1952:90–92).[62] Repetition is a common device, not only in tragedy, but in most serious poetry. Perhaps just this fact discouraged the earlier speech writers from using it: it may have carried the risk of making the

---

[56] For preliterary manifestations, not all of them affective, see Fehling 1969:90–95.

[57] The repetition is, however, not exact insofar as the first syllable is long, then short; and the addition of βροτολοιγέ can place it in the category of "extension of the second member by an epithet" (so Fehling 1969:175).

[58] The extensive treatment in Fehling 1969, as the title indicates, is devoted almost entirely to the period before Gorgias.

[59] *Odyssey* 9.65 is the earliest literary reference to the practice of calling out the name of the dead three times.

[60] Compact statements on exact repetition of words: Schwyzer 1966:699–700 and Wankel 1976 ad Demosthenes *On the Crown* 23. For a discussion of the aesthetic properties of repetition see Stanford 1967:86–93. Rehdantz, commenting ad Demosthenes 2.10, οὐ γὰρ ἔστιν, οὐκ ἔστιν, calls epanadiplosis (or epizeuxis) a means of expressing especially profound emotions; the orator has made his point, but still needs to give vent to his rage.

[61] For instance, at Demosthenes 18.48.3 the thrice-repeated clause opening (μέχρι τούτου), the main verb unit (φίλος ὠνομάζετο) stated once and then to be "supplied" in the next two clauses with different names, and three temporal clauses starting ἕως but with different subjects and verbs.

[62] Worthington 1992:14–39 is far more complimentary.

speaker sound as if he had wandered off the stage of the Theater of Dionysus. Moreover, one meets repetition in tragedy, comedy, and Plato. Though it cannot be shown decisively from any text,[63] it is highly probable that repetition was a feature of colloquial Attic speech, and hence something heard very often in amateur court speech – and hence an *evitandum* until the emergence of a relatively freer dicanic style.

---

[63] Dover ad Aristophanes *Clouds* 1288, πλέον πλέον, compares *Frogs* 1001, μᾶλλον μᾶλλον, and remarks that "the idiom sounds colloquial, and perhaps usually was, but cf. Eur[ipides] *IT* 1406 μᾶλλον δὲ μᾶλλον πρὸς πέτρας ᾔει σκάφος." These expressions, "more and more" and "closer and closer," resemble epanadiplosis, but do not suggest affect.

APPENDIX

THE FORMALITY HYPOTHESIS

A TRADITION STRETCHING BACK TO ANTIQUITY categorizes the earliest preserved Attic oratory as "dignified," "formal," or "austere."[1] In *The Evolution of Greek Prose Style* Dover offers the most precise analysis of this feature and seeks to explain it as a continuation of the traditional style of public speaking at Athens, the only area that has provided specimens suitable for close study. That style avoided various colloquialisms, including features of oral narrative. Most of Dover's evidence is persuasive, but in his treatment of oratory he turns his attention to professional speech exclusively. He does not speculate on (or even mention) amateur speech and does not offer a specific motive for the *logographoi* to retain the basic character of traditional public speech as he reconstructs it from Thucydides, tragedy, and a few other texts.

In arguing for his "hypothesis that the language of early oratory was recognizably formal" Dover adduces Aeschines 1.25, which I quote more fully than he does:

καὶ οὕτως ἦσαν σώφρονες οἱ ἀρχαῖοι ἐκεῖνοι ῥήτορες, ὁ Περικλῆς
καὶ ὁ Θεμιστοκλῆς καὶ ὁ Ἀριστείδης, ὁ τὴν ἀνόμοιον ἔχων ἐπω-
νυμίαν Τιμάρχῳ τουτῳί, ὥστε ὃ νυνὶ πάντες ἐν ἔθει πράττομεν, τὸ

---

[1] The doxography being quite well known, I will mention here only one ancient and one modern (nineteenth-century) opinion linked to it, *exemplorum gratia*. Dionysius of Halicarnassus, in *On Literary Composition* (22.29), chooses Antiphon to represent oratory in a short list of authors who best represent the austere style. Jebb 1876:25, who refers to Dionysius, speaks of "the superb decorum of the old school." To his credit, Jebb leans toward rejection of a moralizing interpretation of the changes that some came along ("It was only when fierce passion and dishonesty had become strong traits of a degenerate national character that vehemence and trickiness came into oratory"). Jebb proposes instead, "It appears simpler to suppose that the conventional stateliness of the old eloquence altogether precluded such vivacity as marked the later; and that the mainspring of the new vivacity was merely the natural impulse, set free from the restraints of the older style, to give arguments their most spirited and effective form" (1876:29).

125

τὴν χεῖρα ἔξω ἔχοντες λέγειν, τότε τοῦτο θρασύ τι ἐδόκει εἶναι καὶ εὐλαβοῦντο αὐτὸ πράττειν.

And those public speakers of old, Pericles and Themistocles and Aristides (who bore a title quite unlike that of this man Timarchus – he was known as "the just") were so decent that in their day this habit that we all practice nowadays, of speaking with the hand outside the clothing, was considered something brash, and they avoided doing it.

Aeschines fatuously stakes his claim on a supposedly archaic statue of Solon,[2] and the other texts he cites (the more or less identical Aristotle *Constitution of the Athenians* 28.3 and Plutarch *Life of Nicias* 8.6) are, as Dover acknowledges, "unsatisfactory" evidence for ancient decorum; but he does regard them as "good evidence for the existence of an ideal by which the actual could be (polemically) judged" (1997:66). As I see it, even the myth of a dignified speech style does not tell us much about the history of the *genos dikanikon*. All the figures supposedly paradigmatic of a restrained style are leading politicians whose best-known speeches would have been largely or exclusively political, not dicanic, and Aeschines refers to them as *rhêtores*, a term that would not apply to the obscure Athenians who found themselves needing to speak in court.[3]

I endorse Dover's insistence that "[f]or the historian, the fact that data of the highest importance [exhibiting the style of symbouleutic and forensic speech prior to about 425] are irrecoverably hidden in darkness is extremely unsatisfactory; but we must never allow that patch of darkness to slip out of our field of vision, never treat what cannot be investigated as if for that reason it did not matter" (1997:60). But it seems to me that, this methodological manifesto notwithstanding, he has not exploited the evidence for the speech of *idiôtai* and the precise motive those men's quotidian speech style gave the *logographoi* for the development and use of a less emotional style.

In one particular I think Dover (1997:63–64) has misinterpreted the data in such a way as to exaggerate the degree to which early professional speech writers reproduced the formality of the tradition: the use or avoid-

---

[2] A piece of pseudo-evidence deflated by Demosthenes (19.251–252). The statue, he says, was created so long after Solon's time that not even the sculptor's grandfather could have laid eyes on Solon.

[3] Note also that in this very encomium of a restrained style Aeschines uses the deictic iota in the word νυνί, a feature that Dover regards as colloquial: see the discussion below.

ance of the long accented iota suffix attached to demonstrative pronouns and several adverbs, usually (at least in the U.S.) referred to as the "deictic iota," but by Dover as the "demonstrative affix -ι" There are no such deictic iotas in Athenian public speech as represented in Thucydides and no credible examples in tragedy (Bers 1997:140 with n36). As Dover shows in his statistical table, the ratio of word tokens to which the deictic iota is added to the same tokens without the suffix is highest in Aristophanes (1:4), lowest in early Platonic dialogues (1:30), quite low in Lysias (1:17), Isocrates (1:28), and Isaeus (1:16), but quite high in Demosthenes (1:7.5). There are several reasons to dispute Dover's conclusions: (1) We can scarcely call the deictic iota rare in the earliest oratory. Antiphon shows the same ratio as Aristophanes, although he is the *logographos* whose language most often among the orators retains conservative features (still using Ionic forms like -σσ, anchoring μέν and δέ with τοῦτο, etc.),[4] preferred οὑτωσί to the word without -ί even more than Aristophanes. Lysias uses νυνί *more* often in proportion to νῦν than Aristophanes. ὡδί makes 14 appearances in Aristophanes and none whatsoever in the canonical orators (a slightly wider group than that canvassed by Dover) other than Demosthenes (12 occurrences), but Andocides is the only orator for whom the TLG shows ὧδε, and in him only once (at 1.25), so it is unlikely that abstention from ὡδί before Demosthenes has any significance. (2) The high frequency of -ί in Aristophanes is very likely to reflect the comic poet's intention to keep his dialogue highly animated.[5]

---

[4] I note a small error in Dover's table: there are three instances of νυνί in Antiphon (5.90; 6.29, 42 – all in actual speeches).

[5] The use of deictic iota is not an Aristophanic tic, but a feature he shares with other comic poets of the fifth century and beyond.

WORKS CITED

Commentaries and Translations with Commentary

Aeschines

Carey, Christopher. 2000. *Aeschines.* The Orators of Classical Greece 3. Austin.
Fisher, Nick. 2001. *Aeschines: Against Timarchos.* Oxford.

Alcidamas

Muir, J. V. 2001. *Alcidamas: The Works and Fragments.* London.

Antiphon

Barigazzi, Adelmo. 1995. *Antifonte: Prima Orazione.* Florence.
Gagarin, Michael. 1997. *Antiphon: The Speeches.* Cambridge.
———. 1998. In Michael Gagarin and Douglas M. MacDowell, *Antiphon and Andocides.* The Orators of Classical Greece 1. Austin.

Andocides

Edwards, Michael. 1995. *Greek Orators IV: Andocides.* Warminster.
MacDowell, Douglas. 1962. *Andocides: On the Mysteries.* Oxford.
———. 1998. In Michael Gagarin and Douglas M. MacDowell, *Antiphon and Andocides.* The Orators of Classical Greece 1. Austin.

Aristophanes

Dover, K. J. 1968a. *Clouds.* Oxford.

Aristotle

Kennedy, George A. 1991. *Aristotle, On Rhetoric: A Theory of Civic Discourse.*
    New York.

Demosthenes

Bers, Victor. 2003. *Demosthenes, Speeches 50–59.* The Orators of Classical Greece
    6. Austin.
Carey, C., and R. A. Reid. 1985. *Demosthenes: Selected Private Speeches.*
    Cambridge.
Paley, F. A., and J. E. Sandys. 1886. *Select Private Orations of Demosthenes, Part I.*
    2nd ed., revised. (Text and commentary on Demosthenes 34, 35, 37, 39,
    40, 56.) Cambridge.
Sandys, J. E., and F. A. Paley. 1896. *Select Private Orations of Demosthenes, Part II.*
    3rd ed., revised. (Text and commentary on Demosthenes 36, 45, 46, 53,
    54, 55.) Cambridge.
Usher, Stephen. 1993. *Demosthenes On the Crown (De corona), Translated with an*
    Introduction and Commentary. Warminster.
Wankel, Hermann. 1976. *Demosthenes: Rede für Ktesiphon über den Kranz.*
    Heidelberg.
Yunis, Harvey. 2001. *Demosthenes On the Crown.* Cambridge.
———. 2005. *Demosthenes, Speeches 18 and 19.* The Orators of Classical
    Greece 9. Austin.

Dinarchus

Worthington, Ian. 1992. *A Historical Commentary on Dinarchus.* Ann Arbor.
———. 2001. In Ian Worthington, Craig Cooper, and Edward M. Harris,
    Dinarchus, Hyperides, and Lycurgus. The Orators of Classical Greece 5.
    Austin.

Hyperides

Cooper, Craig. 2001. In Ian Worthington, Craig Cooper, and Edward M. Harris,
    Dinarchus, Hyperides, and Lycurgus. The Orators of Classical Greece 5.
    Austin.
Whitehead, David. 2000. *Hyperides: The Forensic Speeches.* Oxford.

Isaeus

Edwards, Michael. 2007. *Isaeus.* The Orators of Classical Greece 11.
    Austin, 2007.

Thalheim, T. 1903. Isaeus, *Orationes*. Leipzig.
Wyse, William. 1904. *The Speeches of Isaeus*. Cambridge.

Isocrates

Mirhady, David C., and Yun Lee Too. 2000. *Isocrates I*. The Orators of Classical
Greece 4. Austin.
Papillon, Terry L. 2004. *Isocrates II*. The Orators of Classical Greece 7. Austin.

Lysias

Carey, Christopher. 1989. *Lysias: Selected Speeches*. Cambridge.
Todd, S. C. 2000. *Lysias*. The Orators of Classical Greece 2. Austin.

Plato

Burnet, John. 1924. *Plato's Euthyphro, Apology of Socrates and Crito*. Oxford.
Slings, Simon R., and Emile de Stryker. 1994. *Plato's Apology of Socrates:
A Literary and Philosophical Study with a Running Commentary*. Leiden.

Secondary Works

Allen, Danielle S. 2000. *The World of Prometheus: The Politics of Punishing in
Democratic Athens*. Princeton.
——. 2003. "Angry Bees, Wasps, and Jurors: The Symbolic Politics of ὀργή
in Athens." In Braund and Most 2003:76–98.
Aly, Wolf. 1929. *Formprobleme der frühen griechischen Prosa*. Philologus
Supplementband 21.3. Leipzig.
Bers, Victor. 1984. *Greek Poetic Syntax in the Classical Age*. New Haven.
——. 1985. "Dikastic Thorubos." *Crux: Essays Presented to G.E.M. de Ste. Croix on
his 75th Birthday* (eds. P. A. Cartledge and F. D. Harvey) 1–15. Exeter.
——. 1994. "Tragedy and Rhetoric." *Persuasion: Greek Rhetoric in Action*
(ed. Ian Worthington) 176–195. London.
——. 1997. *Speech in Speech: Studies in Incorporated Oratio Recta in Attic Drama
and Oratory*. Lanham.
Bien, S. M. 1967. "Why Demosthenes Mouthed Pebbles?" *Lancet* 2
(November 25): 1152.
Blass, Friedrich. 1887–98. *Die Attische Beredsamkeit*. 3 vols.; vol 3.1. 2nd ed.
Leipzig.
Boegehold, Alan. 1995. *The Lawcourts at Athens*. The Athenian Agora 28.
Princeton.
Bonner, Robert J. 1927. *Lawyers and Litigants in Ancient Athens*. Chicago.

Braund, Susanna, and Glenn W. Most, eds. 2003. *Ancient Anger: Perspectives from Homer to Galen.* Yale Classical Studies 32. Cambridge.

Carawan. E. M. 1983. "ἐρώτησις: Interrogation in the Courts of Fourth-Century Athens." *GRBS* 24:209–226.

Carey, Christopher. 1994. "Legal Space in Classical Athens." *Greece & Rome* 41:172–186.

———. 1998. "The Shape of Athenian Laws." *CQ* 48:93–109.

———. 1999. "Propriety in the Attic Orators." *Studi sull' eufemismo* (eds. Francesco de Martino and Alan H. Sommerstein) 369–392. Bari.

Cartledge, Paul, Paul Millett, and Sitta von Reden, eds. 1998. *Kosmos: Essays in Order, Conflict and Community in Classical Athens.* Cambridge.

Cassio, A. C. 1981. "Attico 'volgare' e ioni in Athene alla fine del 5. secolo a.C." *Annali dell'Instituto Orientale di Napoli* 6:79–93.

Christ, Matthew R. 1998. *The Litigious Athenian.* Baltimore.

Cole, Thomas. 1991. *The Origins of Rhetoric in Ancient Greece.* Baltimore.

Collard, Christopher. 2005. "Colloquial Language in Tragedy: A Supplement to the Work of P. T. Stevens." *CR* 55:350–386.

Colvin, Stephen. 1997. *Dialect in Aristophanes: The Politics of Language in Ancient Greek Literature.* Oxford.

———. 2000. "The Language of Non-Athenians in Old Comedy." *The Rivals of Aristophanes: Studies in Old Comedy* (eds. David Harvey and John Wilkins) 285–298. London.

Cooper, Craig. 2007. "Forensic Oratory." In Worthington 2007:203–219.

Cribiore, Raffaella. 2001. *Gymnastics of the Mind: Greek Education in Hellenistic and Roman Egypt.* Princeton.

Cucuel. C. 1886. *Essai sur la langue et le style de l'orateur Antiphon.* Paris.

Daitz, Stephen. 1983. "Euripides, Orestes 279 γαλήν' > γαλῆν, or How a Blue Sky Turned into a Pussycat." *CQ* 33:294–295.

Davies. John K. 1981. *Wealth and the Power of Wealth in Classical Athens.* New York.

Denniston. J. D. 1952. *Greek Prose Style.* Oxford.

———. 1954. *The Greek Particles.* 2nd ed. Oxford.

Dessoulavy, P. 1881. *Grammatisch-statistische Beobachtungen über eine Redensart und die Absichtssätze bei den attischen Rednern.* Diss. Würzburg.

Dimock, George E., Jr. 1952. "ἀλλά in Lysias and Plato's Phaedrus." *AJP* 73:381–396.

Dover, K. J. 1950. "The Chronology of Antiphon's Speeches." *CQ* 44:44–60.

———. 1968b. *Lysias and the Corpus Lysiacum.* Berkeley.

———. 1970. "Lo stile di Aristofane." *QUCS* 9:7–23.

———. 1973. K. J. Dover. *Thucydides.* Greece and Rome New Surveys in the Classics 7. Oxford.

———. 1974. *Greek Popular Morality in the Time of Plato and Aristotle.* Oxford.

——. 1975. "Der Stil des Aristophanes." (Translation of Dover 1970 by F. Regen.) *Aristophanes und die alte Kömedie* (ed. H.-J. Newiger) 124–143. Darmstadt.

——. 1981 "The Colloquial Stratum in Classical Attic Prose." *Classical Contributions: Studies in Honour of Malcom Francis McGregor* (eds. G. S. Shrimpton and D. J. McCagar) 15–25. Locust Valley, N.Y.

——. 1985. "Abnormal Word-Order in Attic Comedy." *CQ*, n.s., 35:324–343.

——. 1987. *Greek and the Greeks.* Oxford.

——. 1997. *The Evolution of Greek Prose Style.* Oxford.

Easterling, Pat. 1999. "Actors and Voices: Reading between the Lines in Aeschines and Demosthenes." *Performance Culture and Athenian Democracy* (eds. Simon Goldhill and Robin Osborne) 154–166. Cambridge.

Faraone, Christopher A. 1989. "An Accusation of Magic in Classical Athens (Ar. *Wasps* 946–48)." *TAPA* 119:149–160.

Fehling, Detlev. 1969. *Die Wiederholungsfiguren und ihr Gebrauch bei den Griechen vor Gorgias.* Berlin.

Fisher, Nick. 1998. "Violence, Masculinity and the Law in Classical Athens." *When Men Were Men: Masculinity, Power and Identity in Classical Antiquity* (eds. Lin Foxhall and John Salmon) 68–87. London.

Fraenkel, Eduard. 1962. *Beobachtungen zu Aristophanes.* Rome.

Gagarin, Micahel. 1996. "The Torture of Slaves in Athenian Law." *CP* 91:1–18.

Gay, Peter. 1974. *Style in History.* New York.

Gildersleeve, B. L. 1902. "Problems in Greek Syntax, II." *AJP* 23:121–141.

Gleason, Maud. 1990. "The Semiotics of Gender: Physiognomy and Self-Fashioning in the Second Century C.E." *Before Sexuality: The Construction of Erotic Experience in the Ancient Greek World* (eds. David M. Halperin, John J. Winkler, and Froma I. Zeitlin) 389–415. Princeton.

Glotz, Gustave. 1904. *La solidarité de la famille dans le droit criminel en Grèce.* Paris.

Gluckman, Max. 1965. *The Ideas in Barotse Jurisprudence.* New Haven.

——. 1973. *The Judicial Process among the Barotse of Northern Rhodesia (Zambia).* Reprint of 2nd ed. with minor amendments. Manchester.

Goldhill, Simon. 2002. *The Invention of Prose.* Oxford.

Goodwin, William W. 1890. *Syntax of the Moods and Tenses of the Greek Verb.* Rewritten and enlarged. Boston.

Gould, J. P. 1973. "Hiketeia." *JHS* 93:74–103.

Halliwell, Stephen. 1990. "The Sounds of the Voice in Old Comedy." *Owls to Athens: Essays on Classical Culture Presented to Sir Kenneth Dover* (ed. E. N. Craik) 69–79. Oxford.

——. 2002. *The Aesthetics of Mimesis: Ancient Texts and Modern Problems.* Princeton.

Hansen, M. H. 1975. *Eisangelia: The Sovereignty of the People's Court in Athens in the Fourth Century B.C. and the Impeachment of Generals and Politicians.* Odense.

———. 1979. "How Often Did the Athenian Dicasteria Meet?" *GRBS* 20:243–246.

———. 1984. "Two Notes on Demosthenes' Symbouleutic Speeches." *ClMed* 35:57–70. Republished with addenda in Hansen 1989:283–296.

———. 1989. *The Athenian Ecclesia II: A Collection of Articles, 1983–89.* Copenhagen.

———. 1990. Review of Ober 1989. *CR* 40:348–356.

———. 1999. *The Athenian Democracy in the Age of Demosthenes.* 2nd ed. Norman, Okla.

Harris, Edward M. 2000. "The Authenticity of Andokides' *De Pace.*" *Polis & Politics: Studies in Ancient Greek History Presented to Mogens Herman Hansen on His Sixtieth Birthday* (eds. P. Flensted-Jensen, T. H. Nielsen, and L. Rubinstein) 479–505. Copenhagen.

Harris, William V. 2001. *Restraining Rage: The Ideology of Anger Control in Classical Antiquity.* Cambridge, Mass.

Harrison, A. R. W. 1968. *The Laws of Athens.* 2nd ed. Oxford.

Hawhee, Debra. 2004. *Bodily Arts: Rhetoric and Athletics in Ancient Greece.* Austin.

Henry, Madeleine M. 1995. *Prisoner of History: Aspasia of Miletus and Her Biographical Tradition.* Oxford.

Hesk, Jon. 2000. *Deception and Democracy in Classical Athens.* Cambridge.

Irvine, J. 1984. "Formality and Informality in Communicative Events." *Language in Use: Readings in Sociolinguistics* (eds. John Baugh and Joel Scherzer) 211–228. Englewood Cliffs, N.J.

Jebb, Richard C. 1876. *The Attic Orators from Antiphon to Isaeos.* London.

Johnstone, Steven. 1999. *Disputes and Democracy: The Consequences of Litigation in Ancient Athens.* Austin.

Jong, Irene J. F. de. 1991. *Narrative in Drama: The Art of the Euripidean Messenger-Speech.* Leiden.

Jost, Karl. 1936. *Beispiel und Vorbild der Vorfahren bei den attischen Rednern und Geschichtschreibern bis Demosthenes.* Paderborn.

Keaney, John J. 1974. "Theophrastus on Greek Judicial Procedure." *TAPA* 104:179–184.

Kennedy, George A. 1994. *A New History of Classical Rhetoric.* Princeton.

———. 1998 *Comparative Rhetoric: An Historical and Cross-Cultural Introduction.* New York.

Kermode, Frank. 2000. *Shakespeare's Language.* New York.

———. 2004. *The Age of Shakespeare.* London.

Konstan, David. 2001. *Pity Transformed.* London.

Kühner, Raphael, rev. Bernard Gerth. 1898–1904. *Ausführliche Grammatik der griechischen Sprache.* Part 2: Satzlehre. 2 vols. 3rd ed. Hannover.

Kühnlein, Rudolfus. 1882. *De vi et usu precandi et iurandi formularum apud decem oratores Atticos. Programm der Königliche Studienanstalt zu Neustadt.* Neustadt.

Lanni, Adriaan. 1997. "Spectator Sports or Serious Politics? οἱ περιεστηκότες and the Athenian Lawcourts." *JHS* 117:183–189.

——. 2005. "Relevance in Athenians Courts." *The Cambridge Companion to Ancient Greek Law* (eds. Michael Gagarin and David Cohen) 112–128. Cambridge.

Lavency, M. 1964. *Aspects de la logographie judiciaire attique.* Louvain.

López Eire, A. 1996. *La lengua colloquial de la comedia aristofánica.* Murcia.

MacDowell, D. M. 1963. *Athenian Homicide Law.* Manchester.

——. 1971. "The Chronology of Athenian Speeches and Legal Innovations in 401–398 B.C." *RIDA* 18:267–273.

Macleod, Colin. 1979. "Thucydides on Faction." *PCPS*, n.s., 205:52–68. Reprinted in MacLeod, *Collected Essays* (Oxford, 1983) 123–139.

Markle, M. M., III. 1985. "Jury Pay and Assembly Pay at Athens." *Crux: Essays Presented to G.E.M. de Ste. Croix on his 75th Birthday* (eds. P. A. Cartledge and F. D. Harvey) 265–297. Exeter.

McCabe, Donald F. 1981. *The Prose-Rhythm of Demosthenes.* New York.

Meillet, A. M. 1975. *Aperçu d'une histoire de la langue grecque.* 8th ed. Paris.

North, Helen. 1966. *Sophrosyne: Self-knowledge and Self-restraint in Greek Literature.* Ithaca.

Ober, Josiah. 1989. *Mass and Elite in Democratic Athens.* Princeton.

Ober, Josiah, and Barry Strauss. 1990. "Drama, Political Rhetoric, and the Discourse of Athenian Democracy." *Nothing to Do with Dionysos?* (eds. John Winkler and Froma Zeitlin) 237–270. Princeton.

Opelt, Ilona. 1993. "Schimpfwörter bei den attischen Rednern." *Glotta* 70:227–238.

Osborne, Robin. 1985. "Law in Action in Classical Athens." *JHS* 105:40–58.

Pearson, Lionel. 1976. *The Art of Demosthenes.* Beiträge zur Klassichen Philologie 68. Meisenheim am Glan.

Petersen, Walter. 1910. *Greek Diminutives in -ION: A Study in Semantics.* Weimar.

Pohle, Ulrich. 1928. *Die Sprache des Redners Hypereides in ihren Beziehungen zur Koine.* Klassich-Philologische Studien 2. Leipzig.

Rau, Peter. 1967. *Paratragodia.* Zetemata 45. Munich.

Rhodes, P. J. 1998. "Enmity in Fourth-Century Athens." In Cartledge, Millett, and von Reden 1998:136–153.

Roisman, Joseph. 2005. *The Rhetoric of Manhood: Masculinity in the Attic Orators.* Berkeley.

Rubinstein, Lene. 1998. "The Athenian Political Perception of the *idiotes*." In Cartledge, Millett, and von Reden 1998:125–143.

———. 2000. *Litigation and Cooperation: Supporting Speakers in the Courts of Classical Athens*. Historia Einzelschriften 147. Stuttgart.

———. 2004. "Stirring Up Dicastic Anger." *Law, Rhetoric, and Comedy in Classical Athens: Essays in Honour of Douglas M. MacDowell* (eds. D. L. Cairns and R. A. Knox) 187–204. Swansea.

Rudich, Vasily. 1997. *Dissidence and Literature under Nero: The Price of Rhetoricization*. London.

Scafuro, Adele C. 1997. *The Forensic Stage: Settling Disputes in Graeco-Roman New Comedy*. Cambridge.

Schaeffer, Arnold. 1858. *Demosthenes und seine Zeit*. Leipzig.

Schaps, David. 1977. "The Woman Least Mentioned." *CQ* 27:323–330.

Schmid, Joannes. 1894/95. *De Conviciis a X Oratoribus Atticis Usurpatis*. Programma Gymnasii Ambergensis. Amberg.

Schmid, Wilhelm. 1940. *Geschichte der griechischen Literatur* 1.3. Munich.

Schmidt, Karl Theodor Henry Ludwig. 1891. *De particulae τε earumque quae cum τοι compositae sunt ad oratores Atticos*. Rostock.

Schwyzer, Eduard. 1966. *Griechische Grammatik auf der Grundlage von Karl Brugmanns Griechischer Grammatik*. Vol. 2. Handbuch der Altertumswissenschaft II.1.2. Munich.

Sifakis, G. M. 2002. "The Actor's Art in Aristotle." *Greek and Roman Actors: Aspects of an Ancient Profession* (eds. Pat Easterling and Edith Hall) 148–164. Cambridge.

Smith, Rebekah M. 1994. "Two Fragments of 'Longinus' in Photius." *CQ* 44:525–529.

Sommerstein, Alan H. 1977. Review of Teodorsson 1974. *CR* 27:60–62.

Stahl, Hans-Peter. 1966. *Thucydides: Die Stellung des Menschen im geschichtlichen Prozess*. Munich.

———. 2003. *Thucydides: Man's Place in History*. (Translation of Stahl 1966.) Swansea.

Stanford, W. B. 1967. *The Sound of Greek: Studies in the Greek Theory and Practice of Euphony*. Berkeley.

Taplin, Oliver. 1999. "Spreading the Word through Performance." *Performance Culture and Athenian Democracy* (eds. S. Goldhill and R. Osborne) 33–57. Cambridge.

Teodorsson, Sven-Tage. 1974. *The Phonemic System of the Attic Dialect, 400–340 B.C.* Studia Graeca et Latina Gothoburgensia 32. Lund.

Todd, S. C. 1993. *The Shape of Athenian Law*. Oxford.

Trevett, Jeremy. 1992. *Apollodoros the Son of Pasion*. Oxford.

Usher, Stephen. 1976. "Lysias and His Clients." *GRBS* 17:31–40.

———. 1999. *Greek Oratory: Tradition and Originality*. Oxford.

Wackernagel, Jacob. 1928. *Vorlesungen über Syntax*. 2nd ed. Basel.

Wille, Günther. 2001. *Akroasis: Der akustische Sinnesbereich in der griechischen Literatur bis zum Ende der klassichen Zeit.* Tübingen.

Willi, Andreas. 2003. *The Language of Aristophanes: Aspects of Linguistic Variation in Classical Attic Greek.* Oxford.

Wilson, P. J. 1996. "The Use of Tragedy in the Fourth Century." *Tragedy and the Tragic: Greek Theatre and Beyond* (ed. M. S. Silk) 310–331. Oxford.

Worman, Nancy. 2002. *The Cast of Character.* Austin.

Worthington, Ian, ed. 2007. *A Companion to Greek Rhetoric.* Oxford.

Index Locorum

Index of Greek Words

Subject Index

Achilles, shield of, 27n5

acting style, nineteenth-century, 57n30. *See also* theatricality; tragedy, Attic

Aeschines: on Demosthenes, 38; Demosthenes on, 61, 91; emotionalism of, 36n27; on formality, 125–26; professionalism of, 36n19; prosecution of Ctesiphon, 108n23, 117; prosecution of Timarchus, 52; service as clerk, 63n40; theatricality of, 61–63, 89; use of abusive language, 52; use of exclamations, 113; use of oaths, 108n23, 109; use of *ou mê*, 116–17, 118; use of repetition, 123; use of tragedy, 31; vocal qualities of, 61–62, 63

Aeschylus, oaths in, 110n29

age, stereotypes of, 76n15

amateurs. *See idiôtai*

Anaxagoras, 10n6

Andocides: place in Canon, 36, 52; use of abusive language, 52; use of antithesis, 99n2; use of deictic iota, 127; use of diminutives, 120; use of oaths, 109–10; use of tragic language, 36, 37–38

anger: Aristotle on, 94; Cicero on, 97; in classical literature, 97; displays of, 93–99; use by *idiôtai*, 98

Antiphon, 3; austerity of, 125n1; emotionalism of, 33, 34–35; language of, 46–47; speechwriting by, 13, 14, 35; style of, 35, 125n1; theatricality of, 104; and Thucydides, 33–34; tragic language of, 31–35; use of abusive language, 51, 53n18; use of deictic iota, 127; use of oaths, 109, 114; use of particles, 102, 106

antithesis, in Andocides, 99n2

antitimêsis, 79n2

aphasia: magic spells for, 61; in rhetorical delivery, 60–61

aphelôs, 5

Apollodorus: attacks on Neaera, 52; canonical status of, 7; court speeches of, 3n13; display of emotions, 93n17; feud with Stephanus, 52

Aristogeiton, 121